ROALD DAHL

The Way Up to Heaven
Der Weg zum Himmel

Deutsch von
Wolfheinrich von der Mülbe

D0925463

PONS GmbH
Stuttgart

PONS

ROALD DAHL
The Way Up to Heaven
Der Weg zum Himmel

Deutsch von
Wolfheinrich von der Mülbe

Englischer Originaltext:

"The Way Up To Heaven"
Copyright © 1954 by Roald Dahl Nominee Limited

"Parson's Pleasure"
Copyright © 1959 by Roald Dahl Nominee Limited

Deutsche Übersetzung:

Lizenzausgabe mit freundlicher Genehmigung der
Rowohlt Verlag GmbH, Reinbek bei Hamburg

Entnommen aus: KÜSSCHEN, KÜSSCHEN von Roald Dahl

Copyright © 1953, 1954, 1958, 1959 by Felicity Dahl
and the other Executors of the Estate of Roald Dahl

Copyright © 1962 by Rowohlt Verlag GmbH, Reinbek bei Hamburg

Auflage A1 5 4 3 2 1 / 2012 2011 2010 2009

© PONS GmbH, Rotebühlstraße 77, 70178 Stuttgart, 2008
PONS Produktinfos und Shop: www.pons.de
E-Mail: info@pons.de
Onlinewörterbuch: www.pons.eu
Alle Rechte vorbehalten.

Redaktion: Angelique Slaats, Arkadiusz Wrobel
Redaktionelle Mitarbeit: Karin Adam, Anja Kunzmann
Sprecher / Tonaufnahmen: Mike Cooper (London)
Logoentwurf: Erwin Poell, Heidelberg
Logoüberarbeitung: Sabine Redlin, Ludwigsburg
Titelfoto: shutterstock, Jose Erwin M. Remulla
Einbandgestaltung: Schmidt & Dupont, Stuttgart
Layout: one pm, Petra Michel, Stuttgart
Satz: one pm, Petra Michel, Stuttgart
Druck und Bindung: Print Consult GmbH, München

Printed in Slovak Republic.
ISBN: 978-3-12-561544-1

INHALT

Roald Dahl

DER WEG ZUM HIMMEL

Zeit ihres Lebens hatte Mrs. Foster an einer geradezu pathologischen Angst gelitten, einen Zug, ein Flugzeug, ein Schiff oder den Beginn einer Theatervorstellung zu verpassen. Im allgemeinen war sie gar nicht besonders nervös, aber der bloße Gedanke, sie könnte sich bei solchen Anlässen verspäten, setzte ihr derart zu, daß sie Zuckungen bekam. Es war nicht schlimm – nur eine kleine Muskelreizung im Winkel des linken Auges, wie ein verstohlenes Blinzeln –, doch das Unangenehme war, daß dieser Tic noch mindestens eine Stunde lang anhielt, wenn sie den Zug, das Flugzeug, oder was es nun war, glücklich erreicht hatte.

Merkwürdig, wie sich bei gewissen Leuten eine einfache Besorgnis, zum Beispiel die, den Zug nicht mehr zu erreichen, zu einer Besessenheit auswachsen kann. Spätestens eine halbe Stunde, bevor es Zeit war, zum Bahnhof zu fahren, pflegte Mrs. Foster reisefertig, angetan mit Hut, Mantel und Handschuhen aus dem Aufzug zu treten. Unfähig, sich hinzusetzen, lief sie ziellos von einem Zimmer ins andere, bis ihr Mann, dem ihre Aufregung nicht entgangen sein konnte, endlich zum Vorschein kam und trocken bemerkte, man könne jetzt vielleicht aufbrechen, nicht wahr?

Mr. Foster war durchaus berechtigt, sich über das närrische Benehmen seiner Frau zu ärgern, nicht aber dazu, ihre Qualen zu vergrößern, indem er sie unnötig warten ließ. Daß er das tat, ist zwar durch nichts bewiesen, doch sooft sie zusammen irgendwohin wollten, erschien er unweigerlich im letzten oder vielmehr im allerletzten Moment und benahm sich dabei so betont freundlich, daß die Vermutung sehr nahe lag, er habe seiner unglückseligen Frau ganz bewußt eine boshafte kleine Privatqual auferlegt. Eines jedenfalls mußte ihm klar sein: Sie hätte niemals gewagt, nach ihm zu rufen oder ihn zur Eile anzutreiben. Dazu hatte er sie zu gut erzogen. Und er wußte auch, daß er nur ein klein wenig zu lange zu zögern brauchte, um sie in einen Zustand zu versetzen, der hart an Hysterie grenzte. Bei ein oder zwei besonderen Gelegenheiten in ihren späteren Ehejahren sah es fast so aus, als hätte er den Zug verpassen *wollen*, um die Leiden der armen Frau zu verschlimmern.

Roald Dahl

THE WAY UP TO HEAVEN

All her life, Mrs Foster had had an almost pathological fear of missing a train, a plane, a boat, or even a theatre curtain. In other respects, she was not a particularly nervous woman, but the mere thought of being late on occasions like these would throw her into such a state of nerves that she would begin to twitch. It was nothing much – just a tiny vellicating muscle in the corner of the left eye, like a secret wink – but the annoying thing was that it refused to disappear until an hour or so after the train or plane or whatever it was had been safely caught.

TR. 01

It was really extraordinary how in certain people a simple apprehension about a thing like catching a train can grow into a serious obsession. At least half an hour before it was time to leave the house for the station, Mrs Foster would step out of the elevator all ready to go, with hat and coat and gloves, and then, being quite unable to sit down, she would flutter and fidget about from room to room until her husband, who must have been well aware of her state, finally emerged from his privacy and suggested in a cool dry voice that perhaps they had better get going now, had they not?

Mr Foster may possibly have had a right to be irritated by this foolishness of his wife's, but he could have had no excuse for increasing her misery by keeping her waiting unnecessarily. Mind you, it is by no means certain that this is what he did, yet whenever they were to go somewhere, his timing was so accurate – just a minute or two late, you understand – and his manner so bland that it was hard to believe he wasn't purposely inflicting a nasty private little torture of his own on the unhappy lady. And one thing he must have known – that she would never dare to call out and tell him to hurry. He had disciplined her too well for that. He must also have known that if he was prepared to wait even beyond the last moment of safety, he could drive her nearly into hysterics. On one or two special occasions in the later years of their married life, it seemed almost as though he had *wanted* to miss the train simply in order to intensify the poor woman's suffering.

Genau kann man es ja nicht wissen, aber nimmt man an, daß er schuldig war, so wird sein Verhalten doppelt verwerflich durch die Tatsache, daß ihm Mrs. Foster, abgesehen von dieser einen kleinen Schwäche, immer eine gute und liebevolle Gattin gewesen war. Dreißig Jahre und mehr hatte sie ihm treu und brav gedient. Daran war nicht zu zweifeln. Bei all ihrer Bescheidenheit wußte sie das selbst, und wenn sie sich auch jahrelang gegen den Argwohn gewehrt hatte, Mr. Foster wolle sie absichtlich quälen, so hatte sie sich doch in letzter Zeit mehrmals bei einem beginnenden Zweifel ertappt.

Der nahezu siebzigjährige Mr. Eugen Foster lebte mit seiner Frau in New York City, und zwar in einem großen sechsstöckigen Haus der Zweiundsechzigsten Straße Ost; sie hatten vier Dienstboten. Die Wohnung war ziemlich düster, und sie bekamen nicht viel Besuch. An diesem Januarmorgen aber herrschte im Hause reges Leben und Treiben. Ein Mädchen trug Stapel von Staubhüllen in alle Zimmer, während ein anderes die Tücher über die Möbel breitete. Der Butler brachte die Koffer hinunter und stellte sie in die Halle. Die Köchin kam immer wieder aus der Küche, um mit dem Butler zu reden, und Mrs. Foster selbst, in einem altmodischen Pelzmantel und mit einem schwarzen Hut auf dem Kopf eilte bald hierhin, bald dorthin, angeblich um alles zu überwachen. In Wirklichkeit dachte sie an nichts anderes als daran, daß sie ihr Flugzeug versäumen werde, wenn ihr Mann nicht bald aus seinem Arbeitszimmer käme und sich fertig machte.

«Wie spät ist es, Walker?» fragte sie den Butler.

«Zehn Minuten nach neun, Madam.»

«Ist der Wagen da?»

«Ja, Madam, er wartet. Ich will gerade das Gepäck hinausbringen.»

«Bis Idlewild brauchen wir eine Stunde», sagte sie. «Mein Flugzeug startet um elf, aber wegen der Formalitäten muß ich eine halbe Stunde früher dort sein. Ich werde zu spät kommen. Ich *weiß*, daß ich zu spät kommen werde.»

«Sie schaffen es bequem, Madam», antwortete der Butler beruhigend. «Ich habe Mr. Foster gesagt, daß Sie um neun Uhr fünfzehn hier weg müssen. In fünf Minuten also.»

«Ja, Walker, ich weiß, ich weiß. Aber bitte, beeilen Sie sich mit dem Gepäck, ja?»

Sie ging in der Halle auf und ab, und sooft der Butler vorbeikam, fragte sie ihn, wie spät es sei. Dabei wiederholte sie sich immer von neuem, daß sie gerade dieses Flugzeug nicht versäumen dürfe. Monate hatte sie gebraucht, ihrem Mann die Erlaubnis zur Reise abzuringen. Kam sie zu spät, so verlangte er womöglich, sie solle ihr Vorhaben aufgeben. Das Schlimme war, daß er darauf bestand, sie zum Flugplatz zu begleiten.

Assuming (though one cannot be sure) that the husband was guilty, what made his attitude doubly unreasonable was the fact that, with the exception of this one small irrepressible foible, Mrs Foster was and always had been a good and loving wife. For over thirty years, she had served him loyally and well. There was no doubt about this. Even she, a very modest woman, was aware of it, and although she had for years refused to let herself believe that Mr Foster would ever consciously torment her, there had been times recently when she had caught herself beginning to wonder.

Mr Eugene Foster, who was nearly seventy years old, lived with his wife in a large six-storey house in New York City, on East Sixty-second Street, and they had four servants. It was a gloomy place, and few people came to visit them. But on this particular morning in January, the house had come alive and there was a great deal of bustling about. One maid was distributing bundles of dust sheets to every room, while another was draping them over the furniture. The butler was bringing down suitcases and putting them in the hall. The cook kept popping up from the kitchen to have a word with the butler, and Mrs Foster herself, in an old-fashioned fur coat and with a black hat on the top of her head, was flying from room to room and pretending to supervise these operations. Actually, she was thinking of nothing at all except that she was going to miss her plane if her husband didn't come out of his study soon and get ready.

TR. 02

'What time is it, Walker?' she said to the butler as she passed him.

'It's ten minutes past nine, Madam.'

'And has the car come?'

'Yes, Madam, it's waiting. I'm just going to put the luggage in now.'

'It takes an hour to get to Idlewild,' she said. 'My plane leaves at eleven. I have to be there half an hour beforehand for the formalities. I shall be late. I just *know* I'm going to be late.'

'I think you have plenty of time, Madam,' the butler said kindly. 'I warned Mr Foster that you must leave at nine-fifteen. There's still another five minutes.'

'Yes, Walker, I know, I know. But get the luggage in quickly, will you please?'

She began walking up and down the hall, and whenever the butler came by, she asked him the time. This, she kept telling herself, was the *one* plane she must not miss. It had taken months to persuade her husband to allow her to go. If she missed it, he might easily decide that she should cancel the whole thing. And the trouble was that he insisted on coming to the airport to see her off.

«Guter Gott», sagte sie laut, «ich komme zu spät. Ich weiß, ich weiß, ich *weiß*, daß ich zu spät komme.» Der kleine Muskel am linken Auge zuckte bereits heftig. Die Augen selbst waren dicht am Weinen.

«Wie spät ist es, Walker?»

«Achtzehn Minuten nach, Madam.»

«Jetzt verpasse ich es ganz bestimmt!» rief sie. «Wenn er doch nur käme!»

Für Mrs. Foster war diese Reise sehr wichtig. Sie wollte allein nach Paris fliegen, um ihre Tochter, ihr einziges Kind, zu besuchen, die mit einem Franzosen verheiratet war. Für den Franzosen hatte Mrs. Foster nicht viel übrig, aber sie liebte ihre Tochter, und vor allem sehnte sie sich danach, endlich einmal ihre drei Enkel zu sehen. Sie kannte sie nur von den vielen Fotos, die sie erhalten hatte und die überall in der Wohnung aufgestellt waren. Entzückende Kinder. Mrs. Foster hing mit einer wahren Affenliebe an ihnen, und sooft ein neues Bild kam, zog sie sich damit zurück, betrachtete es lange und liebevoll und suchte in den kleinen Gesichtern nach den befriedigenden Kennzeichen der Blutsverwandtschaft, die so viel bedeutet. In letzter Zeit war ihr immer stärker zum Bewußtsein gekommen, daß sie keinen Wert darauf legte, den Rest ihres Lebens an einem Ort zu verbringen, wo sie diese Kinder nicht in ihrer Nähe haben, sie besuchen, auf Spaziergänge mitnehmen, beschenken, aufwachsen sehen konnte. Natürlich wußte sie, daß es falsch und gewissermaßen pflichtvergessen war, solche Gedanken zu hegen, solange ihr Mann lebte. Und ebenso wußte sie, daß Mr. Foster – obgleich er sich nicht mehr in seinen vielen Unternehmungen betätigte – niemals einwilligen würde, New York zu verlassen und nach Paris zu übersiedeln. Es war schon ein Wunder, daß er ihr gestattet hatte, für sechs Wochen hinüberzufliegen und ihre Lieben zu besuchen. Ach, wie sie wünschte, immer bei ihnen leben zu können!

«Wie spät, Walker?»

«Zweiundzwanzig Minuten nach, Madam.»

Der Butler hatte noch nicht zu Ende gesprochen, als die Tür aufging und Mr. Foster in die Halle trat. Er blieb einen Moment stehen, den Blick auf seine Frau gerichtet, und auch sie sah ihn an, den kleinen, noch immer hübschen alten Mann, dessen Gesicht mit dem gewaltigen Bart den bekannten Fotografien von Andrew Carnegie verblüffend ähnelte.

«Nun», sagte er, «ich glaube, wir sollten wohl langsam aufbrechen, wenn du das Flugzeug noch erreichen willst.»

«Ja, Lieber – ja! Es ist alles bereit. Der Wagen wartet.»

«Gut.» Er neigte den Kopf ein wenig zur Seite und musterte sie aufmerksam.

'Dear God,' she said aloud, 'I'm going to miss it. I know, I know, I *know* I'm going to miss it.' The little muscle beside the left eye was twitching madly now. The eyes themselves were very close to tears.

'What time is it, Walker?'

'It's eighteen minutes past, Madam.'

'Now I really *will* miss it!' she cried. 'Oh, I wish he would come!'

TR. 03

This was an important journey for Mrs Foster. She was going all alone to Paris to visit her daughter, her only child, who was married to a Frenchman. Mrs Foster didn't care much for the Frenchman, but she was fond of her daughter, and, more than that, she had developed a great yearning to set eyes on her three grandchildren. She knew them only from the many photographs that she had received and that she kept putting up all over the house. They were beautiful, these children. She doted on them, and each time a new picture arrived she would carry it away and sit with it for a long time, staring at it lovingly and searching the small faces for signs of that old satisfying blood likeness that meant so much. And now, lately, she had come more and more to feel that she did not really wish to live out her days in a place where she could not be near these children, and have them visit her, and take them for walks, and buy them presents, and watch them grow. She knew, of course, that it was wrong and in a way disloyal to have thoughts like these while her husband was still alive. She knew also that although he was no longer active in his many enterprises, he would never consent to leave New York and live in Paris. It was a miracle that he had ever agreed to let her fly over there alone for six weeks to visit them. But, oh, how she wished she could live there always, and be close to them!

'Walker, what time is it?'

'Twenty-two minutes past, Madam.'

TR. 04

As he spoke, a door opened and Mr Foster came into the hall. He stood for a moment, looking intently at his wife, and she looked back at him – at this diminutive but still quite dapper old man with the huge bearded face that bore such an astonishing resemblance to those old photographs of Andrew Carnegie.

'Well,' he said, 'I suppose perhaps we'd better get going fairly soon if you want to catch that plane.'

'*Yes*, dear – *yes!* Everything's ready. The car's waiting.'

'That's good,' he said. With his head over to one side, he was watching

Diese Angewohnheit, den Kopf schräg zu legen und ihn dann in kleinen, schnellen Rucken zu bewegen, war charakteristisch für ihn. Deswegen und weil er die Hände in Brusthöhe zu verschränken pflegte, erinnerte er, wenn er so dastand, an ein Eichhörnchen, ein nettes, lebhaftes Eichhörnchen aus dem Park.

«Hier ist Walker mit deinem Mantel, Lieber. Zieh ihn an.» «Ich muß mir noch die Hände waschen», sagte er. «Bin gleich zurück.»

Sie wartete, während der Buller Hut und Mantel bereithielt. «Meinen Sie, daß ich zu spät komme, Walker?»

«Nein, Madam», erwiderte der Butler, «Sie schaffen es bestimmt.»

Als Mr. Foster erschien, half ihm der Butler in den Mantel. Mrs. Foster eilte hinaus und stieg in den gemieteten Cadillac. Ihr Mann folgte ihr, ging aber die Stufen vor der Haustür sehr gemächlich hinunter und blieb auf halbem Wege stehen, um den Himmel zu betrachten und die kalte Morgenluft zu schnuppern.

«Sieht ein bißchen neblig aus», meinte er, als er sich im Wagen neben sie setzte. «Und draußen in Idlewild ist es meistens noch schlimmer. Ich würde mich nicht wundern, wenn gar keine Flugzeuge starten dürften.»

«Sag das nicht, Lieber – *bitte.*»

Sie schwiegen beide, bis der Wagen den Fluß überquert und Long Island erreicht hatte.

«Mit den Dienstboten habe ich alles geordnet», sagte Mr. Foster. «Sie gehen heute weg. Ich habe ihnen für sechs Wochen den halben Lohn gegeben und Walker gesagt, daß ich ihm telegrafieren werde, wenn wir sie wieder benötigen.»

«Ja», antwortete sie. «Er hat's mir erzählt.»

«Ich ziehe heute abend in den Klub. Wird zur Abwechslung mal ganz nett sein, im Klub zu wohnen.»

«Ja, Lieber, und ich werde dir schreiben.»

«Ab und zu schaue ich dann zu Hause nach, ob alles in Ordnung ist, und hole die Post.»

«Meinst du nicht, daß Walker doch lieber die ganze Zeit dableiben sollte, um nach dem Rechten zu sehen?» fragte sie zaghaft.

«Unsinn. Ganz überflüssig. Und ich müßte ihm dann den vollen Lohn zahlen.»

«Ach ja, natürlich.»

«Außerdem weiß man nie, was die Leute anstellen, wenn sie allein im Hause sind», verkündete Mr. Foster. Er zog eine Zigarre heraus, knipste die Spitze mit einem silbernen Zigarrenabschneider ab und ließ sein goldenes Feuerzeug aufflammen.

her closely. He had a peculiar way of cocking the head and then moving it in a series of small, rapid jerks. Because of this and because he was clasping his hands up high in front of him, near the chest, he was somehow like a squirrel standing there – a quick clever old squirrel from the Park.

'Here's Walker with your coat, dear. Put it on.'

'I'll be with you in a moment,' he said. 'I'm just going to wash my hands.'

She waited for him, and the tall butler stood beside her, holding the coat and the hat. 'Walker, will I miss it?'

'No, Madam,' the butler said. 'I think you'll make it all right.'

Then Mr Foster appeared again, and the butler helped him on with his coat. Mrs Foster hurried outside and got into the hired Cadillac. Her husband came after her, but he walked down the steps of the house slowly, pausing halfway to observe the sky and to sniff the cold morning air.

'It looks a bit foggy,' he said as he sat down beside her in the car. 'And it's always worse out there at the airport. I shouldn't be surprised if the flight's cancelled already.'

'Don't say that, dear – *please*.'

They didn't speak again until the car had crossed over the river to Long Island.

'I arranged everything with the servants,' Mr Foster said. 'They're all going off today. I gave them half-pay for six weeks and told Walker I'd send him a telegram when we wanted them back.'

'Yes,' she said. 'He told me.'

'I'll move into the club tonight. It'll be a nice change staying at the club.'

'Yes, dear. I'll write to you.'

'I'll call in at the house occasionally to see that everything's all right and to pick up the mail.'

'But don't you really think Walker should stay there all the time to look after things?' she asked meekly.

'Nonsense. It's quite unnecessary. And anyway, I'd have to pay him full wages.'

'Oh yes,' she said. 'Of course.'

'What's more, you never know what people get up to when they're left alone in a house,' Mr Foster announced, and with that he took out a cigar and, after snipping off the end with a silver cutter, lit it with a gold lighter.

Seine Frau saß regungslos neben ihm, die Hände unter der Decke zusammengekrampft.

«Wirst du mir schreiben?» fragte sie.

«Mal sehen», antwortete er. «Ich glaub's aber nicht. Du weißt, ich schreibe nicht gern Briefe, wenn nichts Besonderes mitzuteilen ist.»

«Ja, Lieber, ich weiß. Mach's, wie du willst.»

Sie fuhren weiter, den Queens Boulevard entlang, und als sie sich dem flachen Marschland näherten, auf dem Idlewild erbaut ist, wurde der Nebel dichter, und der Wagen mußte das Tempo verlangsamen.

«Oh!» rief Mrs. Foster. «Jetzt werde ich das Flugzeug *bestimmt* verpassen! Wie spät ist es?»

«Reg dich nicht auf», sagte der alte Mann. «Ob du zur Zeit kommst oder nicht, spielt gar keine Rolle. Das Flugzeug kann ohnehin nicht starten. Bei solchem Wetter fliegen sie nie. Ich begreife nicht, warum du überhaupt losgefahren bist.»

Täuschte sie sich, oder hatte seine Stimme plötzlich einen neuen Klang? Sie wandte sich ihm zu. Die vielen Haare machten es schwierig, eine Veränderung in seinem Gesichtsausdruck wahrzunehmen. Das wichtigste war der Mund. Wie schon so oft, wünschte sie sich, ihn deutlich sehen zu können. Seine Augen verrieten nie etwas, ausgenommen, wenn er zornig war.

«Natürlich», fuhr er fort, «falls das Flugzeug zufällig doch startet, kommst du zu spät – darin muß ich dir zustimmen. Wäre es nicht besser, gleich umzukehren?»

Sie antwortete nicht und schaute durch das Fenster nach dem Nebel. Je weiter sie kamen, desto dichter schien er zu werden; sie konnte gerade den Straßenrand erkennen und ein wenig Grasland. Sie spürte, daß ihr Mann sie noch immer beobachtete. Auch sie sah ihn nun an, und dabei stellte sie mit einer Art Entsetzen fest, daß er unverwandt auf die Stelle in ihrem linken Augenwinkel blickte, wo sie den Muskel zucken fühlte.

«Nun?» sagte er.

«Was denn?»

«Wenn das Flugzeug startet, erreichst du es bestimmt nicht mehr. Bei dem Nebel können wir nicht schnell fahren.»

Nach diesen Worten hüllte er sich in Schweigen. Der Wagen kroch dahin. Der Fahrer hielt eine gelbe Lampe auf den Straßenrand gerichtet, und das half ihm weiter. Andere Lichter, weiße oder gelbe, tauchten vor ihnen aus dem Nebel auf, und ein besonders helles folgte ihnen die ganze Zeit.

Plötzlich hielt der Fahrer an.

She sat still in the car with her hands clasped together tight under the rug.

'Will you write to me?' she asked.

'I'll see,' he said. 'But I doubt it. You know I don't hold with letter-writing unless there's something specific to say.'

'Yes, dear, I know. So don't you bother.'

They drove on, along Queen's Boulevard, and as they approached the flat marshland on which Idlewild is built, the fog began to thicken and the car had to slow down.

'Oh dear!' cried Mrs Foster. 'I'm *sure* I'm going to miss it now! What time is it?'

'Stop fussing,' the old man said. 'It doesn't matter anyway. It's bound to be cancelled now.

They never fly in this sort of weather. I don't know why you bothered to come out.'

She couldn't be sure, but it seemed to her that there was suddenly a new note in his voice, and she turned to look at him. It was difficult to observe any change in his expression under all that hair. The mouth was what counted. She wished, as she had so often before, that she could see the mouth clearly. The eyes never showed anything except when he was in a rage.

'Of course,' he went on, 'if by any chance it *does* go, then I agree with you – you'll be certain to miss it now. Why don't you resign yourself to that?'

She turned away and peered through the window at the fog. It seemed to be getting thicker as they went along, and now she could only just make out the edge of the road and the margin of grassland beyond it. She knew that her husband was still looking at her. She glanced at him again, and this time she noticed with a kind of horror that he was staring intently at the little place in the corner of her left eye where she could feel the muscle twitching.

'Won't you?' he said.

'Won't I what?'

'Be sure to miss it now if it goes. We can't drive fast in this muck.'

He didn't speak to her any more after that. The car crawled on and on. The driver had a yellow lamp directed on to the edge of the road, and this helped him to keep going. Other lights, some white and some yellow, kept coming out of the fog towards them, and there was an especially bright one that followed close behind them all the time.

Suddenly, the driver stopped the car.

«So!» rief Mr. Foster. «Jetzt sitzen wir fest. Wundert mich gar nicht.»

Der Fahrer drehte sich um. «Nein, Sir, wir haben's geschafft. Dies ist der Flughafen.»

Mrs. Foster sprang wortlos aus dem Wagen und eilte zum Haupteingang. In der Halle belagerten zahlreiche Menschen, meist verzweifelte Reisende, die Schalter. Sie bahnte sich einen Weg durch die Menge und befragte den Angestellten.

«Ja», sagte er, «der Abflug ist verschoben worden. Aber gehen Sie bitte nicht weg. Das Wetter kann sich jeden Augenblick aufklären.»

Sie kehrte zu ihrem Mann zurück, der noch immer im Wagen saß, und erzählte ihm die Neuigkeit. «Du brauchst wirklich nicht zu warten, Lieber», fügte sie hinzu. «Das hätte keinen Sinn.»

«Ich warte auch nicht», sagte er. «Vorausgesetzt, daß der Chauffeur mich zurückfahren kann. Wird das möglich sein, Chauffeur?»

«Ich denke, ja», meinte der Mann.

«Ist das Gepäck abgeladen?»

«Ja, Sir.»

«Leb wohl, Lieber.» Mrs. Foster beugte sich in den Wagen und gab ihrem Mann einen raschen Kuß auf den stachligen grauen Pelz seiner Wange.

«Leb wohl», antwortete er. «Gute Reise.»

Der Wagen verschwand im Nebel, und Mrs. Foster blieb allein zurück.

Der Rest des Tages war eine Art Alpdruck für sie. Stunde um Stunde saß sie auf einer Bank, möglichst nahe bei dem Schalter der Fluggesellschaft, und etwa alle dreißig Minuten stand sie auf, um zu fragen, ob sich irgend etwas geändert habe. Immer erhielt sie die gleiche Antwort – sie müsse weiter warten, weil sich der Nebel jeden Augenblick lichten könne. Erst nach sechs Uhr abends gaben die Lautsprecher bekannt, der Abflug sei auf elf Uhr am nächsten Vormittag verlegt worden.

Als Mrs. Foster das hörte, wußte sie sich keinen Rat. Sie saß noch mindestens eine halbe Stunde auf ihrer Bank und dachte müde und verwirrt darüber nach, wo sie die Nacht verbringen sollte. Den Flugplatz zu verlassen, hatte sie keine Lust. Ihren Mann zu sehen auch nicht. Sie fürchtete, es werde ihm irgendwie gelingen, ihre Reise nach Frankreich zu hintertreiben. Am liebsten wäre sie geblieben, wo sie war: auf der Bank. Von allen Lösungen war dies die sicherste. Aber Mrs. Foster war erschöpft, und zudem wurde ihr klar, daß sie, eine ältere Dame, sich damit lächerlich machen würde. So ging sie denn schließlich in eine Telefonzelle und rief zu Hause an.

'There!' Mr Foster cried. 'We're stuck. I knew it.'

'No, sir,' the driver said, turning round. 'We made it. This is the airport.'

Without a word, Mrs Foster jumped out and hurried through the main entrance into the building. There was a mass of people inside, mostly disconsolate passengers standing around the ticket counters. She pushed her way through and spoke to the clerk.

'Yes,' he said. 'Your flight is temporarily postponed. But please don't go away. We're expecting this weather to clear any moment.'

She went back to her husband who was still sitting in the car and told him the news. 'But don't you wait, dear,' she said. 'There's no sense in that.'

'I won't,' he answered. 'So long as the driver can get me back. Can you get me back, driver?'

'I think so,' the man said.

'Is the luggage out?'

'Yes, sir.'

'Good-bye, dear,' Mrs Foster said, leaning into the car and giving her husband a small kiss on the coarse grey fur of his cheek.

'Good-bye,' he answered. 'Have a good trip.'

The car drove off, and Mrs Foster was left alone.

The rest of the day was a sort of nightmare for her. She sat for hour after hour on a bench, as close to the airline counter as possible, and every thirty minutes or so she would get up and ask the clerk if the situation had changed. She always received the same reply – that she must continue to wait, because the fog might blow away at any moment. It wasn't until after six in the evening that the loudspeakers finally announced that the flight had been postponed until eleven o'clock the next morning.

TR. 05

Mrs Foster didn't quite know what to do when she heard this news. She stayed sitting on her bench for at least another half-hour, wondering, in a tired, hazy sort of way, where she might go to spend the night. She hated to leave the airport. She didn't wish to see her husband. She was terrified that in one way or another he would eventually manage to prevent her from getting to France. She would have liked to remain just where she was, sitting on the bench the whole night through. That would be the safest. But she was already exhausted, and it didn't take her long to realize that this was a ridiculous thing for an elderly lady to do. So in the end she went to a phone and called the house.

Ihr Mann, der gerade in den Klub fahren wollte, meldete sich. Sie berichtete ihm, was geschehen war, und fragte, ob die Dienstboten noch dort seien.

«Die sind alle weg», antwortete er.

«Dann werde ich mir ein Hotelzimmer nehmen. Du brauchst dich keinesfalls um mich zu kümmern.»

«Das wäre verrückt», entgegnete er. «Hier hast du doch das ganze Haus zu deiner Verfügung.»

«Aber, mein Lieber, es ist *leer.*»

«Dann bleibe ich eben bei dir.»

«Wir haben auch nichts zu essen im Hause. Nichts.»

«Iß, bevor du kommst. Sei nicht so dumm. Du bist wirklich das unbeholfenste Geschöpf, das mir je begegnet ist.»

«Ja», sagte sie. «Es tut mir leid. Ich werde hier ein Sandwich essen und dann kommen.»

Draußen hatte sich der Nebel ein wenig gelichtet, aber sie mußte trotzdem eine lange, langsame Taxifahrt überstehen und traf erst sehr spät in der Zweiundsechzigsten Straße ein.

Ihr Mann öffnete die Tür seines Arbeitszimmers, als er ihren Schritt hörte. «Nun?» fragte er von der Schwelle her. «Wie war's in Paris?»

«Ich fliege morgen früh um elf», antwortete sie. «Endgültig.» «Du meinst, wenn sich der Nebel verzieht.» «Er verzieht sich jetzt schon. Es ist Wind aufgekommen.»

«Du siehst müde aus», sagte er. «Du hattest gewiß einen unruhigen Tag.»

«Sehr angenehm war's nicht. Ich denke, ich gehe gleich zu Bett.»

«Ich habe für morgen um neun einen Wagen bestellt.»

«Ach, vielen Dank, Lieber. Und ich hoffe wirklich, du wirst dir nicht die Mühe machen, wieder mit hinauszufahren.»

«Nein», sagte er langsam. «Ich glaube nicht, daß ich mitkommen werde. Aber eigentlich könntest du mich unterwegs im Klub absetzen.»

Sie schaute ihn an und hatte plötzlich das Gefühl, er stehe weit weg von ihr, jenseits irgendeiner Grenze. Er wirkte so klein, so entfernt, daß sie nicht recht wußte, was er tat, was er dachte oder auch nur, was er war.

«Der Klub ist in der City», wandte sie ein. «Das ist nicht die Richtung zum Flugplatz.»

«Du hast reichlich Zeit, meine Liebe. Oder magst du mir den Gefallen nicht tun?»

«Doch, natürlich.»

«Dann ist ja alles in Ordnung. Wir sehen uns morgen früh um neun.»

Her husband, who was on the point of leaving for the club, answered it himself. She told him the news, and asked whether the servants were still there.

'They've all gone,' he said.

'In that case, dear, I'll just get myself a room somewhere for the night. And don't you bother yourself about it at all.'

'That would be foolish,' he said. 'You've got a large house here at your disposal. Use it.'

'But, dear, it's *empty*.'

'Then I'll stay with you myself.'

'There's no food in the house. There's nothing.'

'Then eat before you come in. Don't be so stupid, woman. Everything you do, you seem to want to make a fuss about it.'

'Yes,' she said. 'I'm sorry. I'll get myself a sandwich here, and then I'll come on in.'

Outside, the fog had cleared a little, but it was still a long, slow drive in the taxi, and she didn't arrive back at the house on Sixty-second Street until fairly late.

Her husband emerged from his study when he heard her coming in. 'Well,' he said, standing by the study door, 'how was Paris?'

'We leave at eleven in the morning,' she answered. 'It's definite.'

'You mean if the fog clears.'

'It's clearing now. There's a wind coming up.'

'You look tired,' he said. 'You must have had an anxious day.'

'It wasn't very comfortable. I think I'll go straight to bed.'

'I've ordered a car for the morning,' he said. 'Nine o'clock.'

'Oh, thank you, dear. And I certainly hope you're not going to bother to come all the way out again to see me off.'

'No,' he said slowly. 'I don't think I will. But there's no reason why you shouldn't drop me at the club on your way.'

She looked at him, and at that moment he seemed to be standing a long way off from her, beyond some borderline. He was suddenly so small and far away that she couldn't be sure what he was doing, or what he was thinking, or even what he was.

'The club is downtown,' she said. 'It isn't on the way to the airport.'

'But you'll have plenty of time, my dear. Don't you want to drop me at the club?'

'Oh, yes – of course.'

'That's good. Then I'll see you in the morning at nine.'

Sie ging in ihr Zimmer im zweiten Stock und war so erschöpft von den Anstrengungen dieses Tages, daß sie sofort einschlief.

Am nächsten Morgen stand Mrs. Foster zeitig auf, und um halb neun war sie bereits reisefertig.

Kurz nach neun erschien ihr Mann. «Hast du Kaffee gemacht?» fragte er.

«Nein», antwortete sie. «Ich dachte, du würdest im Klub ein gutes Frühstück bekommen. Der Wagen ist da. Er wartet schon eine ganze Weile.»

Sie standen in der Halle – neuerdings schienen sie sich immer in der Halle zu treffen –, sie in Hut und Mantel, die Handtasche über dem Arm, er in einem altmodischen Jackett mit breiten Aufschlägen.

«Dein Gepäck?»

«Das ist auf dem Flugplatz.»

«Ach ja», sagte er, «natürlich. Wenn du mich zuerst in den Klub bringen willst, dann sollten wir wohl lieber gleich aufbrechen, wie?»

«Ja!» rief sie. «O ja – bitte!»

«Ich hole mir nur noch ein paar Zigarren. Geh ruhig schon vor, ich komme sofort nach.»

Sie drehte sich um und eilte hinaus. Der Chauffeur öffnete ihr die Wagentür.

«Wie spät ist es?» fragte sie ihn.

«Ungefähr neun Uhr fünfzehn.»

Fünf Minuten darauf kam Mr. Foster. Er stieg langsam die Stufen hinunter, und seine Frau stellte fest, daß er in den engen Röhrenhosen, die er trug, Beine wie ein Ziegenbock hatte. Wie tags zuvor blieb er auf halbem Wege stehen, schnupperte die Luft und betrachtete den Himmel. Wenn auch das Wetter noch nicht ganz klar war, so drangen doch ein paar Sonnenstrahlen durch den Dunst.

«Vielleicht hast du diesmal mehr Glück», meinte er und kletterte in den Wagen.

«Beeilen Sie sich, bitte», sagte sie zu dem Chauffeur. «Halten Sie sich nicht mit der Decke auf. Das mache ich schon. Bitte fahren Sie, wir haben uns ohnehin verspätet.»

Der Mann setzte sich hinter das Lenkrad und ließ den Motor an. «Moment mal», meldete sich Mr. Foster plötzlich. «Warten Sie einen Augenblick, Chauffeur, ja?»

«Was ist denn, Lieber?» Sie sah ihn in seinen Manteltaschen wühlen.

«Ich hatte ein kleines Geschenk, das du Ellen mitbringen solltest», sagte er. «Herrje, wo ist es denn nur? Ich weiß genau, daß ich's in der Hand hatte, als ich in die Halle kam.»

«Mir ist gar nicht aufgefallen, daß du etwas trugst. Was für ein Geschenk?»

She went up to her bedroom on the second floor, and she was so exhausted from her day that she fell asleep soon after she lay down.

Next morning, Mrs Foster was up early, and by eight-thirty she was downstairs and ready to leave.

Shortly after nine, her husband appeared. 'Did you make any coffee?' he asked.

'No, dear. I thought you'd get a nice breakfast at the club. The car is here. It's been waiting. I'm all ready to go.'

They were standing in the hall – they always seemed to be meeting in the hall nowadays – she with her hat and coat and purse, he in a curiously cut Edwardian jacket with high lapels.

'Your luggage?'

'It's at the airport.'

'Ah yes,' he said. 'Of course. And if you're going to take me to the club first, I suppose we'd better get going fairly soon, hadn't we?'

'Yes!' she cried. 'Oh, yes – *please!*'

'I'm just going to get a few cigars. I'll be right with you. You get in the car.'

She turned and went out to where the chauffeur was standing, and he opened the car door for her as she approached. 'What time is it?' she asked him. 'About nine-fifteen.'

Mr Foster came out five minutes later, and watching him as he walked slowly down the steps, she noticed that his legs were like goat's legs in those narrow stovepipe trousers that he wore. As on the day before, he paused halfway down to sniff the air and to examine the sky. The weather was still not quite clear, but there was a wisp of sun coming through the mist.

'Perhaps you'll be lucky this time,' he said as he settled himself beside her in the car.

'Hurry, please,' she said to the chauffeur. 'Don't bother about the rug. I'll arrange the rug. Please get going. I'm late.'

The man went back to his seat behind the wheel and started the engine.

'*Just* a moment!' Mr Foster said suddenly. 'Hold it a moment, chauffeur, will you?'

'What is it, dear?' She saw him searching the pockets of his overcoat.

'I had a little present I wanted you to take to Ellen,' he said. 'Now, where on earth is it? I'm sure I had it in my hand as I came down.'

'I never saw you carrying anything. What sort of present?'

«Eine kleine, in weißes Papier gewickelte Schachtel. Ich habe gestern vergessen, sie dir zu geben. Heute möchte ich es nicht wieder vergessen.»

«Eine kleine Schachtel!» rief Mrs.Foster. «Ich habe keine kleine Schachtel gesehen!» Sie suchte fieberhaft auf den Wagensitzen herum. Ihr Mann kramte weiter in seinen Taschen. Dann knöpfte er den Mantel auf und tastete sein Jackett ab. «Zu dumm», sagte er. «Ich muß es im Schlafzimmer gelassen haben. Warte, ich bin sofort wieder da.»

«Bitte!» flehte sie. «Wir haben keine Zeit! Bitte, laß es! Du kannst es schicken. Es ist ja doch nur ein alberner Kamm. Du schenkst ihr immer Kämme.»

«Und was hast du gegen Kämme, wenn ich fragen darf?» Er war wütend, weil sie sich so hatte gehenlassen.

«Gar nichts, mein Lieber. Gewiß nicht. Aber ...»

«Warte hier», befahl er. «Ich hole die Schachtel.»

«Mach schnell, Lieber! Bitte, mach schnell!»

Sie saß im Wagen und wartete und wartete.

«Chauffeur, wie spät ist es?»

Der Mann schaute auf seine Armbanduhr. «Gleich halb zehn.»

«Schaffen wir's in einer Stunde bis zum Flughafen?»

«Ja, mit knapper Not.»

In diesem Augenblick entdeckte Mrs.Foster plötzlich die Ecke von etwas Weißem, das zwischen Sitz und Lehne eingekeilt war, dort, wo ihr Mann gesessen hatte. Sie zog ein in Papier gewickeltes Päckchen heraus und stellte unwillkürlich fest, daß es so tief im Polster steckte, als hätte eine Hand nachgeholfen.

«Hier ist es!» rief sie. «Ich hab's gefunden! Oje, und nun sucht er da oben alles durch! Chauffeur, rasch – laufen Sie hinein und rufen Sie ihn, wenn Sie so gut sein wollen!»

Dem Chauffeur, einem Mann mit einem trotzigen, schmallippigen irischen Mund, paßte das alles nicht recht, aber er stieg aus und ging die Stufen zur Haustür hinauf. Gleich darauf kam er zurück. «Die Tür ist zu», sagte er. «Haben Sie den Schlüssel?»

«Ja, einen Moment ...» Sie kramte wild in ihrer Handtasche. Ihr kleines Gesicht war vor Angst verzerrt, der Mund krampfhaft zusammengepreßt.

«Hier! Nein – ich gehe selbst. Das ist besser. Ich weiß, wo er ist.»

Sie sprang aus dem Wagen und eilte die Stufen hinauf, den Schlüssel in der Hand. Schon hatte sie ihn ins Schlüsselloch gesteckt, war im Begriff, ihn zu drehen – da hielt sie inne. Sie hob den Kopf und stand vollständig regungslos, wie erstarrt

'A little box wrapped up in white paper. I forgot to give it to you yesterday. I don't want to forget it today.'

'A little box!' Mrs Foster cried. 'I never saw any little box!' She began hunting frantically in the back of the car.

Her husband continued searching through the pockets of his coat. Then he unbuttoned the coat and felt around in his jacket. 'Confound it,' he said, 'I must've left it in my bedroom. I won't be a moment.'

'Oh, *please!*' she cried. 'We haven't got time! *Please* leave it! You can mail it. It's only one of those silly combs anyway. You're always giving her combs.'

'And what's wrong with combs, may I ask?' he said, furious that she should have forgotten herself for once.

'Nothing, dear, I'm sure. But ...'

'Stay here!' he commanded. 'I'm going to get it.'

'Be quick, dear! Oh, *please* be quick!'

She sat still, waiting and waiting.

'Chauffeur, what time is it?'

The man had a wristwatch, which he consulted. 'I make it nearly nine-thirty.'

'Can we get to the airport in an hour?'

'Just about.'

At this point, Mrs Foster suddenly spotted a corner of something white wedged down in the crack of the seat on the side where her husband had been sitting. She reached over and pulled out a small paper-wrapped box, and at the same time she couldn't help noticing that it was wedged down firm and deep, as though with the help of a pushing hand.

'Here it is!' she cried. 'I've found it! Oh dear, and now he'll be up there for ever searching for it! Chauffeur, quickly – run in and call him down, will you please?'

The chauffeur, a man with a small rebellious Irish mouth, didn't care very much for any of this, but he climbed out of the car and went up the steps to the front door of the house. Then he turned and came back. 'Door's locked,' he announced. 'You got a key?'

'Yes – wait a minute.' She began hunting madly in her purse. The little face was screwed up tight with anxiety, the lips pushed outward like a spout.

'Here it is! No – I'll go myself. It'll be quicker. I know where he'll be.'

She hurried out of the car and up the steps to the front door, holding the key in one hand. She slid the key into the keyhole and was about to turn it – and then she stopped. Her head came up, and she stood there absolutely motionless,

inmitten all der Hast, die Tür zu öffnen und das Haus zu betreten. Sie wartete – fünf Sekunden, sechs, sieben, acht, neun, zehn. Wie sie da stand, mit erhobenem Kopf und angespanntem Körper, schien sie zu lauschen, ob sich ein Laut wiederholen werde, den sie soeben aus dem Innern des Hauses gehört hatte.

Ja, sie lauschte – das war offensichtlich. Ihre ganze Haltung drückte Lauschen aus. Man sah förmlich, wie sie ihr Ohr immer näher an die Tür brachte. Nun lag es unmittelbar an dem Holz, und sekundenlang behielt sie diese Stellung bei: den Kopf erhoben, das Ohr an der Tür, den Schlüssel in der Hand, bereit einzutreten, aber doch nicht eintretend und statt dessen offenbar bemüht, die schwachen Laute zu analysieren, die aus dem Innern des Hauses drangen.

Auf einmal kam wieder Leben in Mrs. Foster. Sie zog den Schlüssel aus der Tür, machte kehrt und rannte zum Wagen zurück.

«Es ist zu spät!» rief sie dem Chauffeur zu. «Ich kann nicht auf ihn warten, ich kann einfach nicht, weil ich sonst das Flugzeug versäume. Fahren Sie, Chauffeur, rasch! Zum Flugplatz!»

Hätte der Mann sie genau betrachtet, so wäre ihm zweifellos aufgefallen, daß sie kreidebleich geworden war und daß sich ihr Gesichtsausdruck plötzlich verändert hatte. Keine Spur mehr von ihrem sanften, ziemlich einfältigen Blick. Eine merkwürdige Härte hatte sich über ihre Züge verbreitet. Der kleine, sonst so schlaffe Mund war schmal und fest, die Augen blitzten, und als sie sprach, klang aus ihrer Stimme eine ungewohnte Autorität.

«Schnell, Chauffeur, schnell!»

«Reist denn Ihr Mann nicht mit Ihnen?» fragte er erstaunt.

«O nein, ich wollte ihn nur im Klub absetzen, aber das ist jetzt nicht wichtig. Er wird's schon einsehen und sich ein Taxi nehmen. Reden Sie nicht so lange. *Fahren Sie! Ich muß die Maschine nach Paris erreichen!*»

Unaufhörlich von Mrs. Foster angetrieben, fuhr der Mann wie die Feuerwehr, so daß er sie einige Minuten vor dem Start des Flugzeugs in Idlewild absetzen konnte. Bald war sie hoch über dem Atlantik, behaglich in ihren Sessel gelehnt, dem Motorengebrumm lauschend, in Gedanken schon in Paris. Noch immer befand sie sich in dieser neuen Stimmung. Sie fühlte sich ungemein kräftig und empfand ein eigenartiges Wohlbehagen. Wenn sie ein wenig atemlos war, so kam das mehr von der Verwunderung über das, was sie getan hatte, als von sonst etwas, und während sich das Flugzeug immer weiter von New York und der Zweiundsechzigsten Straße entfernte, senkte sich eine große Ruhe auf sie herab. Bei der Ankunft in Paris war sie so frisch, kühl und gelassen, wie sie es sich nur wünschen konnte.

her whole body arrested right in the middle of all this hurry to turn the key and get into the house, and she waited – five, six, seven, eight, nine, ten seconds, she waited. The way she was standing there, with her head in the air and the body so tense, it seemed as though she were listening for the repetition of some sound that she had heard a moment before from a place far away inside the house.

Yes – quite obviously she was listening. Her whole attitude was a *listening* one. She appeared actually to be moving one of her ears closer and closer to the door. Now it was right up against the door, and for still another few seconds she remained in that position, head up, ear to door, hand on key, about to enter but not entering, trying instead, or so it seemed, to hear and to analyse these sounds that were coming faintly from this place deep within the house.

Then, all at once, she sprang to life again. She withdrew the key from the door and came running back down the steps.

'It's too late!' she cried to the chauffeur. 'I can't wait for him, I simply can't. I'll miss the plane. Hurry now, driver, hurry! To the airport!'

The chauffeur, had he been watching her closely, might have noticed that her face had turned absolutely white and that the whole expression had suddenly altered. There was no longer that rather soft and silly look. A peculiar hardness had settled itself upon the features. The little mouth, usually so flabby, was now tight and thin, the eyes were bright, and the voice, when she spoke, carried a new note of authority.

'Hurry, driver, hurry!'

'Isn't your husband travelling with you?' the man asked, astonished.

'Certainly not! I was only going to drop him at the club. It won't matter. He'll understand. He'll get a cab. Don't sit there talking, man. *Get going!* I've got a plane to catch for Paris!'

With Mrs Foster urging him from the back seat, the man drove fast all the way, and she caught her plane with a few minutes to spare. Soon she was high up over the Atlantic, reclining comfortably in her aeroplane chair, listening to the hum of the motors, heading for Paris at last. The new mood was still with her. She felt remarkably strong and, in a queer sort of way, wonderful. She was a trifle breathless with it all, but this was more from pure astonishment at what she had done than anything else, and as the plane flew farther and farther away from New York and East Sixty-second Street, a great sense of calmness began to settle upon her. By the time she reached Paris, she was just as strong and cool and calm as she could wish.

TR. 07

Sie lernte ihre Enkelkinder kennen und fand sie in Fleisch und Blut noch viel schöner als auf den Fotos. Wie Engel, sagte sie sich, wie Engel sind sie! Und jeden Tag ging sie mit ihnen spazieren, fütterte sie mit Kuchen, kaufte ihnen Geschenke und erzählte ihnen wunderhübsche Geschichten.

Einmal in der Woche, am Dienstag, schrieb sie ihrem Mann einen netten Plauderbrief, voll von Neuigkeiten und Klatsch, den sie stets mit den Worten schloß: «Und bitte, achte darauf, daß Du regelmäßig ißt, obgleich ich befürchte, Du wirst das nicht tun, solange ich weg bin.»

Als die sechs Wochen um waren, bedauerten alle, daß sie nach Amerika zurückkehren mußte. Alle, nur sie nicht. Merkwürdigerweise schien ihr das nicht soviel auszumachen, wie man hätte erwarten können, und als sie ihre Lieben zum Abschied küßte, deutete irgend etwas in ihrem Verhalten und in ihren Worten auf die Möglichkeit hin, daß sie in nicht allzu ferner Zukunft wiederkommen werde.

Pflichtgetreu, wie sie war, hielt sie sich streng an das vereinbarte Datum. Genau sechs Wochen nach ihrer Ankunft schickte sie ihrem Mann ein Kabel und bestieg die Maschine nach New York.

In Idlewild stellte Mrs. Foster mit Interesse fest, daß kein Wagen auf sie wartete. Vielleicht amüsierte sie das sogar ein wenig. Sie war jedoch sehr ruhig und gab dem Träger, der ihr Gepäck zum Taxi schaffte, kein übertrieben hohes Trinkgeld.

In New York war es kälter als in Paris, und an den Straßenrändern lagen schmutzige Schneehaufen. Das Taxi hielt vor dem Haus in der Zweiundsechzigsten Straße, und Mrs. Foster überredete den Chauffeur, ihre beiden großen Koffer bis zur Haustür zu tragen. Dann bezahlte sie ihn und läutete. Sie wartete, aber niemand kam. Sicherheitshalber drückte sie noch einmal auf den Knopf. Sie hörte die Glocke im hinteren Teil des Hauses schrillen, doch nichts rührte sich.

So nahm sie denn ihren eigenen Schlüssel und schloß auf.

Das erste, was sie bei ihrem Eintritt erblickte, war ein Berg von Briefen, die auf dem Boden lagen, wie sie durch den Türschlitz gefallen waren. In der Halle war es dunkel und kalt. Über der alten Uhr hing eine Staubhülle. Trotz der Kälte war die Luft merkwürdig drückend, und Mrs. Foster spürte einen schwachen eigentümlichen Geruch, den sie nie zuvor wahrgenommen hatte.

Mit schnellen Schritten durchquerte sie die Halle und bog hinten links um die Ecke. In ihren Bewegungen war etwas Energisches und Zielbewußtes; sie wirkte wie eine Frau, die einer Sache auf den Grund gehen, die Bestätigung eines Verdachts

She met her grandchildren, and they were even more beautiful in the flesh than in their photographs. They were like angels, she told herself, so beautiful they were. And every day she took them for walks, and fed them cakes, and bought them presents, and told them charming stories.

Once a week, on Tuesdays, she wrote a letter to her husband – a nice, chatty letter – full of news and gossip, which always ended with the words 'Now be sure to take your meals regularly, dear, although this is something I'm afraid you may not be doing when I'm not with you.'

When the six weeks were up, everybody was sad that she had to return to America, to her husband. Everybody, that is, except her. Surprisingly, she didn't seem to mind as much as one might have expected, and when she kissed them all good-bye, there was something in her manner and in the things she said that appeared to hint at the possibility of a return in the not too distant future.

However, like the faithful wife she was, she did not overstay her time. Exactly six weeks after she had arrived, she sent a cable to her husband and caught the plane back to New York.

Arriving at Idlewild, Mrs Foster was interested to observe that there was no car to meet her. It is possible that she might even have been a little amused. But she was extremely calm and did not overtip the porter who helped her into a taxi with her baggage.

TR. 08

New York was colder than Paris, and there were lumps of dirty snow lying in the gutters of the streets. The taxi drew up before the house on Sixty-second Street, and Mrs Foster persuaded the driver to carry her two large cases to the top of the steps. Then she paid him off and rang the bell. She waited, but there was no answer. Just to make sure, she rang again, and she could hear it tinkling shrilly far away in the pantry, at the back of the house. But still no one came.

So she took out her own key and opened the door herself.

The first thing she saw as she entered was a great pile of mail lying on the floor where it had fallen after being slipped through the letter box. The place was dark and cold. A dust sheet was still draped over the grandfather clock. In spite of the cold, the atmosphere was peculiarly oppressive, and there was a faint and curious odour in the air that she had never smelled before.

She walked quickly across the hall and disappeared for a moment around the corner to the left, at the back. There was something deliberate and purposeful about this action; she had the air of a woman who is off to investigate

suchen will. Und als sie nach ein paar Sekunden zurückkam, lag auf ihrem Gesicht ein kleiner Schimmer von Befriedigung.

Mitten in der Halle blieb sie stehen, als dächte sie darüber nach, was sie nun tun solle. Dann drehte sie sich mit einem Ruck um und ging in das Arbeitszimmer ihres Mannes. Auf dem Schreibtisch lag ein Notizbuch. Sie blätterte eine Weile darin, nahm dann den Telefonhörer ab und stellte eine Verbindung her.

«Hallo», sagte sie, «hören Sie hier ist Nummer neun, Zweiundsechzigste Straße Ost ... Ja, ganz recht. Könnten Sie wohl sobald wie möglich jemanden herüberschicken? Ja, er ist steckengeblieben, vermutlich zwischen der zweiten und der dritten Etage. Das ist jedenfalls der Stand, den der Anzeiger angibt ... Sofort? Ach, das ist sehr freundlich von Ihnen. Wissen Sie, für meine Beine ist das viele Treppensteigen nichts mehr. Recht schönen Dank. Auf Wiederhören.»

Sie legte auf, blieb an dem Schreibtisch ihres Mannes sitzen und wartete geduldig auf den Monteur, der den Aufzug reparieren sollte.

a rumour or to confirm a suspicion. And when she returned a few seconds later, there was a little glimmer of satisfaction on her face.

She paused in the centre of the hall, as though wondering what to do next. Then, suddenly, she turned and went across into her husband's study. On the desk she found his address book, and after hunting through it for a while she picked up the phone and dialled a number.

'Hello,' she said. 'Listen – this is Nine East Sixty-second Street … Yes, that's right. Could you send someone round as soon as possible, do you think? Yes, it seems to be stuck between the second and third floors. At least, that's where the indicator's pointing … Right away? Oh, that's very kind of you. You see, my legs aren't any too good for walking up a lot of stairs. Thank you so much. Good-bye.'

She replaced the receiver and sat there at her husband's desk, patiently waiting for the man who would be coming soon to repair the lift.

Roald Dahl

DES PFARRERS FREUDE

Mr. Boggis fuhr langsam dahin, behaglich zurückgelehnt, den Ellbogen auf den Rahmen des offenen Wagenfensters gestützt. Eine herrliche Gegend, dachte er, und wie erfreulich es ist, die ersten Boten des Sommers zu sehen. Vor allem die Schlüsselblumen, den Weißdorn und den Rotdorn. Die Hecken standen in voller Blüte, weiß, rosa und rot; darunter leuchteten in kleinen Büscheln die gelben Schlüsselblumen, und das war wunderschön.

Er ließ das Lenkrad mit einer Hand los und zündete sich eine Zigarette an. Am besten fahre ich jetzt den Brill Hill hinauf, beschloß er. Der Hügel lag vor ihm, etwa eine halbe Meile entfernt. Und das da mußte das Dorf Brill sein, diese in Grün eingebettete Gruppe ländlicher Häuser auf dem Gipfel. Ausgezeichnet. Nicht oft fand er bei seinen Sonntagsunternehmungen ein so günstig gelegenes Arbeitsgebiet.

Oben auf dem Hügel brachte er den Wagen am Rande des Dorfes zum Stehen, stieg aus und hielt Umschau. Wie ein riesiger grüner Teppich breitete sich die Landschaft vor ihm aus. Er konnte meilenweit sehen. Sehr gut war das. Er zog einen Block und einen Bleistift aus der Tasche, lehnte sich an den Wagen und ließ seinen geübten Blick langsam in die Runde schweifen.

Zur Rechten entdeckte er inmitten der Felder ein mittelgroßes Bauernhaus, zu dem von der Landstraße her ein Weg führte. Dahinter stand ein größeres. Dann war da ein von hohen Ulmen umgebenes Haus, das aus der Zeit Queen Annes stammen mochte, und auch die beiden Bauernhöfe, die weiter nach links lagen, sahen vielversprechend aus. Insgesamt also fünf. Das war wohl alles auf dieser Seite.

Mr. Boggis zeichnete in groben Zügen einen Lageplan auf seinen Block, damit er die Häuser nachher mühelos wiederfinden konnte. Dann stieg er in seinen Wagen und fuhr durch das Dorf auf die andere Seite des Hügels. Von dort erspähte er sechs weitere Möglichkeiten – fünf Höfe und ein großes weißes Haus in georgianischem Stil. Es sah sauber und gepflegt aus, auch der Garten war in bester Ordnung. Schade. Er schaltete es sofort aus. Zu wohlhabenden Leuten zu gehen hatte gar keinen Sinn.

Roald Dahl

PARSON'S PLEASURE

TR. 01

Mr Boggis was driving the car slowly, leaning back comfortably in the seat with one elbow resting on the sill of the open window. How beautiful the country-side, he thought; how pleasant to see a sign or two of summer once again. The primroses especially. And the hawthorn. The hawthorn was exploding white and pink and red along the hedges and the primroses were growing under-neath in little clumps, and it was beautiful.

He took one hand off the wheel and lit himself a cigarette. The best thing now, he told himself, would be to make for the top of Brill Hill. He could see it about half a mile ahead. And that must be the village of Brill, that cluster of cottages among the trees right on the very summit. Excellent. Not many of his Sunday sections had a nice elevation like that to work from.

He drove up the hill and stopped the car just short of the summit on the out-skirts of the village. Then he got out and looked around. Down below, the country-side was spread out before him like a huge green carpet. He could see for miles. It was perfect. He took a pad and pencil from his pocket, leaned against the back of the car, and allowed his practised eye to travel slowly over the landscape.

He could see one medium farmhouse over on the right, back in the fields, with a track leading to it from the road. There was another larger one beyond it. There was a house surrounded by tall elms that looked as though it might be a Queen Anne, and there were two likely farms away over on the left. Five places in all. That was about the lot in this direction.

Mr Boggis drew a rough sketch on his pad showing the position of each so that he'd be able to find them easily when he was down below, then he got back into the car and drove up through the village to the other side of the hill. From there he spotted six more possibles – five farms and one big white Georgian house. He studied the Georgian house through his binoculars. It had a clean prosperous look, and the garden was well ordered. That was a pity. He

29

Mithin blieben alles in allem zehn Versuchsobjekte. Zehn ist eine hübsche Zahl, sagte sich Mr. Boggis. Gerade richtig für eine gemächliche Nachmittagsarbeit. Wie spät war es jetzt? Elf Uhr. Eigentlich hätte er ja gern ein Glas Bier getrunken, bevor er anfing, aber sonntags wurden die Wirtshäuser erst um zwölf geöffnet. Na schön, dann eben später. Er warf einen Blick auf seinen Plan und entschied sich für das Queen-Anne-Haus, das mit den Ulmen. Durchs Fernglas hatte es so hübsch verfallen ausgesehen. Die Bewohner würden vermutlich etwas Geld gut gebrauchen können. Mit Queen-Anne-Häusern hatte er von jeher Glück gehabt. Mr. Boggis klemmte sich hinter das Lenkrad, löste die Handbremse und ließ den Wagen ohne Motor langsam den Hügel hinunterrollen.

Abgesehen davon, daß er im Augenblick als Geistlicher verkleidet war, gab es an Mr. Cyril Boggis nichts auszusetzen. Er war Antiquitätenhändler, hatte sich auf Möbel spezialisiert und besaß in Chelsea, in der King's Road, einen Laden mit Ausstellungsraum. Sein Lager war nicht groß, und die Geschäfte gingen nicht allzu gut, doch da er immer billig einkaufte, sehr, sehr billig sogar, und sehr, sehr teuer verkaufte, brachte er es doch fertig, jedes Jahr einen netten kleinen Verdienst herauszuschlagen. Er war äußerst gewandt und hatte die Gabe, beim Kaufen wie beim Verkaufen genau den Ton anzuschlagen, der ihm die Sympathie des jeweiligen Kunden gewann: ernst, aber charmant für die Bejahrten, untertänig für die Reichen, schlicht für die Frommen, herrisch für die Weichen, mutwillig für die Witwen, frech und schelmisch für die alten Jungfern. Dieses Talentes war er sich durchaus bewußt, und er machte bei jeder Gelegenheit schamlos davon Gebrauch. Nach einer besonders gut geglückten Darbietung konnte er sich manchmal kaum enthalten, einen Schritt vorzutreten und sich zu verbeugen, als hätte ihm ein unsichtbares Publikum donnernden Applaus gespendet.

Trotz dieser ziemlich hanswurstmäßigen Eigenschaft war Mr. Boggis beileibe kein Narr. Man sagte ihm sogar nach, er verstehe von französischem, englischem und italienischem Mobiliar ebensoviel wie die besten Experten in London. Er hatte einen überraschend sicheren Geschmack, und wenn ihm ein Stück mißfiel, lehnte er es ohne Zögern ab, so echt es auch sein mochte. Seine eigentliche Liebe gehörte natürlich den Werken der großen englischen Kunsttischler und Architekten des achtzehnten Jahrhunderts – Ince, Mayhew, Chippendale, Robert Adam, Manwaring, Inigo Jones, Hepplewhite, Kent, Johnson, George Smith, Lock, Sheraton und wie sie alle heißen –, doch auch hier zog er gelegentlich eine Grenze. In seinem Ausstellungsraum duldete er zum Beispiel kein einziges Stück aus Chippendales chinesischer oder gotischer Periode, und ebenso verwarf er einige der massigeren italienischen Entwürfe von Robert Adam.

ruled it out immediately. There was no point in calling on the prosperous.

In this square then, in this section, there were ten possibles in all. Ten was a nice number, Mr Boggis told himself. Just the right amount for a leisurely afternoon's work. What time was it now? Twelve o'clock. He would have liked a pint of beer in the pub before he started, but on Sundays they didn't open until one. Very well, he would have it later. He glanced at the notes on his pad. He decided to take the Queen Anne first, the house with the elms. It had looked nicely dilapidated through the binoculars. The people there could probably do with some money. He was always lucky with Queen Annes, anyway. Mr Boggis climbed back into the car, released the handbrake, and began cruising slowly down the hill without the engine.

Apart from the fact that he was at this moment disguised in the uniform of a clergyman, there was nothing very sinister about Mr Cyril Boggis. By trade he was a dealer in antique furniture, with his own shop and showroom in the King's Road, Chelsea. His premises were not large, and generally he didn't do a great deal of business, but because he always bought cheap, very very cheap, and sold very very dear, he managed to make quite a tidy little income every year. He was a talented salesman, and when buying or selling a piece he could slide smoothly into whichever mood suited the client best. He could become grave and charming for the aged, obsequious for the rich, sober for the godly, masterful for the weak, mischievous for the widow, arch and saucy for the spinster. He was well aware of his gift, using it shamelessly on every possible occasion; and often, at the end of an unusually good performance, it was as much as he could do to prevent himself from turning aside and taking a bow or two as the thundering applause of the audience went rolling through the theatre.

TR. 02

In spite of this rather clownish quality of his, Mr Boggis was not a fool. In fact, it was said of him by some that he probably knew as much about French, English, and Italian furniture as anyone else in London. He also had surprisingly good taste, and he was quick to recognize and reject an ungraceful design, however genuine the article might be. His real love, naturally, was for the work of the great eighteenth-century English designers, Ince, Mayhew, Chippendale, Robert Adam, Manwaring, Inigo Jones, Hepplewhite, Kent, Johnson, George Smith, Lock, Sheraton, and the rest of them, but even with these he occasionally drew the line. He refused, for example, to allow a single piece from Chippendale's Chinese or Gothic period to come into his showroom, and the same was true of some of the heavier Italian designs of Robert Adam.

Durch sein Geschick, mit erstaunlicher Regelmäßigkeit ungewöhnliche, oft sogar sehr seltene Gegenstände aufzustöbern, hatte sich Mr. Boggis in den letzten Jahren beträchtlichen Ruhm bei seinen Geschäftsfreunden erworben. Anscheinend verfügte der Mann über eine nahezu unerschöpfliche Quelle, eine Art privaten Warenlagers, aus dem er sich von Woche zu Woche versorgte. Fragte man ihn, woher er die Sachen beziehe, so lächelte er überlegen und murmelte etwas von einem kleinen Geheimnis.

Hinter Mr. Boggis' kleinem Geheimnis steckte eine höchst einfache Idee. Sie ging auf ein Erlebnis zurück, das er vor nahezu neun Jahren gehabt hatte, als er eines Sonntagnachmittags über Land fuhr. Er hatte sich am Morgen aufgemacht, um seine Mutter in Sevenoaks zu besuchen, und auf dem Rückweg war irgend etwas mit dem Kühler passiert, so daß sich der Motor überhitzte und das Wasser wegkochte. Er war ausgestiegen, zum nächsten Haus gegangen, einem Bauernhäuschen, etwa fünfzig Schritt von der Straße entfernt, und hatte die Frau, die ihm öffnete, um einen Krug Wasser gebeten.

Während er auf ihre Rückkehr vom Brunnen wartete, warf er zufällig einen Blick durch die offene Tür ins Wohnzimmer, und dort, greifbar nahe, entdeckte er so etwas Aufregendes, daß ihm der Schweiß auf die Stirn trat. Es war ein großer eichener Armstuhl von besonderer Art – so einen hatte er erst einmal im Leben gesehen. Jeder Arm wie auch die Fläche der Rückenlehne ruhte auf acht wundervoll gedrechselten Spindeln. Die Rückenlehne selbst war mit einer Einlegearbeit verziert, einem herrlichen Blumenmuster, und ein geschnitzter Entenkopf nahm die Hälfte jeder der beiden Armstützen ein. Guter Gott, dachte Mr. Boggis, das ist ja spätes fünfzehntes Jahrhundert!

Er steckte den Kopf weiter durch die Tür, und siehe da, auf der anderen Seite des Kamins stand wahrhaftig noch so ein Sessel!

Ganz sicher wußte er es nicht, aber zwei Stühle wie diese waren in London mindestens tausend Pfund wert. Ach, und wie schön sie waren!

Als die Frau zurückkam, stellte Mr. Boggis sich vor und fragte ohne Umschweife, ob sie die Sessel vielleicht verkaufen wolle.

«Du meine Güte», sagte sie, «warum in aller Welt sollte ich meine Sessel verkaufen?»

Aus keinem anderen Grunde, als weil er bereit sei, ihr ein schönes Stück Geld dafür zu bezahlen.

Tatsächlich? Wieviel denn? Sie denke zwar nicht daran zu verkaufen, aber aus Neugier, so zum Spaß, wissen Sie – wieviel würde er geben?

«Fünfunddreißig Pfund.» –

During the past few years, Mr Boggis had achieved considerable fame among his friends in the trade by his ability to produce unusual and often quite rare items with astonishing regularity. Apparently the man had a source of supply that was almost inexhaustible, a sort of private warehouse, and it seemed that all he had to do was to drive out to it once a week and help himself. Whenever they asked him where he got the stuff, he would smile knowingly and wink and murmur something about a little secret.

The idea behind Mr Boggis's little secret was a simple one, and it had come to him as a result of something that had happened on a certain Sunday afternoon nearly nine years before, while he was driving in the country.

TR. 03

He had gone out in the morning to visit his old mother, who lived in Sevenoaks, and on the way back the fanbelt on his car had broken, causing the engine to overheat and the water to boil away. He had got out of the car and walked to the nearest house, a smallish farm building about fifty yards off the road, and had asked the woman who answered the door if he could please have a jug of water.

While he was waiting for her to fetch it, he happened to glance in through the door to the living-room, and there, not five yards from where he was standing, he spotted something that made him so excited the sweat began to come out all over the top of his head. It was a large oak armchair of a type that he had only seen once before in his life. Each arm, as well as the panel at the back, was supported by a row of eight beautifully turned spindles. The back panel itself was decorated by an inlay of the most delicate floral design, and the head of a duck was carved to lie along half the length of either arm. Good God, he thought. This thing is late fifteenth century!

He poked his head in further through the door, and there, by heavens, was another of them on the other side of the fireplace!

He couldn't be sure, but two chairs like that must be worth at least a thousand pounds up in London. And oh, what beauties they were!

When the woman returned, Mr Boggis introduced himself and straight away asked if she would like to sell her chairs.

Dear me, she said. But why on earth should she want to sell her chairs?

No reason at all, except that he might be willing to give her a pretty nice price.

And how much would he give? They were definitely not for sale, but just out of curiosity, just for fun, you know, how much would he give?

Thirty-five pounds.

«Wieviel?»

«Fünfunddreißig Pfund.»

Lieber Himmel, fünfunddreißig Pfund. Ja, ja, das sei sehr interessant. Für wertvoll habe sie die Stühle immer gehalten. Sie seien sehr alt. Und außerdem sehr bequem. Aber sie könne sie unmöglich entbehren, auf keinen Fall. Nein, da sei leider nichts zu machen. Trotzdem vielen Dank.

In Wirklichkeit, erklärte Mr. Boggis, seien die Sessel gar nicht so alt und daher auch keineswegs leicht zu verkaufen; er habe jedoch gerade einen Kunden an der Hand, der solche Sachen liebe. Vielleicht könne er noch zwei Pfund zulegen – sagen wir siebenunddreißig. Wie wäre es damit?

Eine halbe Stunde lang ging der Handel hin und her. Zuletzt bekam Mr. Boggis natürlich die Sessel und bezahlte dafür kaum den zwanzigsten Teil ihres Wertes.

Als Mr. Boggis am Abend nach London zurückfuhr – die beiden Prachtstücke waren im hinteren Teil des alten Kombiwagens untergebracht –, kam ihm plötzlich ein Gedanke, den er für glänzend hielt.

Sieh einmal, sagte er sich, wenn in diesem Bauernhaus gute Sachen sind, warum dann nicht auch in anderen? Sollte man also nicht danach suchen? Alle ländlichen Bezirke durchkämmen? Sonntags, zum Beispiel, weil es dann nicht bei der Arbeit stört ... Mit dem Sonntag wußte Mr. Boggis ohnehin nie etwas anzufangen.

Er kaufte Landkarten, Karten in großem Maßstab von allen Grafschaften rund um London, und teilte sie mit einer feinen Feder in Quadrate ein, deren jedes ein Gebiet von fünf zu fünf Meilen umfaßte. Soviel konnte er seiner Schätzung nach bei gründlichem Vorgehen an einem Sonntag erledigen. Städte und große Dörfer wollte er außer acht lassen und lieber abgelegene Ortschaften, Bauernhöfe und mehr oder weniger verfallene Herrensitze aufsuchen. Wenn er allsonntäglich ein Quadrat abklapperte, zweiundfünfzig im Jahr, würde er nach und nach jeden Hof und jedes Bauernhaus der näheren und weiteren Umgebung erfassen.

Offensichtlich war es aber damit noch nicht getan. Landleute sind eine mißtrauische Gesellschaft. Ebenso die verarmten Reichen. Man kann nicht einfach an ihre Tür klopfen und erwarten, daß sie einem das ganze Haus zeigen, nur weil man es gern besichtigen möchte. Das tun sie nicht. Auf die Weise kommt man noch nicht einmal über die Schwelle. Wie sollte man sich also Einlaß verschaffen? Vielleicht war es am besten, gar nicht zu sagen, daß man Händler war. Man konnte sich als Telefonmann ausgeben, als Klempner, als Beauftragter der Gasanstalt. Oder als Geistlicher ...

Damit bekam der Plan Hand und Fuß. Mr. Boggis ließ eine Menge Visitenkarten drucken, auf denen zu lesen stand:

How much?

Thirty-five pounds.

Dear me, thirty-five pounds. Well, well, that was very interesting. She'd always thought they were valuable. They were very old. They were very comfortable too. She couldn't possibly do without them, not possibly. No, they were not for sale but thank you very much all the same.

They weren't really so very old, Mr Boggis told her, and they wouldn't be at all easy to sell, but it just happened that he had a client who rather liked that sort of thing. Maybe he could go up another two pounds – call it thirty-seven. How about that?

They bargained for half an hour, and of course in the end Mr Boggis got the chairs and agreed to pay her something less than a twentieth of their value.

That evening, driving back to London in his old station-wagon with the two fabulous chairs tucked away snugly in the back, Mr Boggis had suddenly been struck by what seemed to him to be a most remarkable idea.

Look here, he said. If there is good stuff in one farmhouse, then why not in others? Why shouldn't he search for it? Why shouldn't he comb the countryside? He could do it on Sundays. In that way, it wouldn't interfere with his work at all. He never knew what to do with his Sundays.

So Mr Boggis bought maps, large-scale maps of all the counties around London, and with a fine pen he divided each of them up into a series of squares. Each of these squares covered an actual area of five miles by five, which was about as much territory, he estimated, as he could cope with on a single Sunday, were he to comb it thoroughly. He didn't want the towns and the villages. It was the comparatively isolated places, the large farmhouses and the rather dilapidated country mansions, that he was looking for; and in this way, if he did one square each Sunday, fifty-two squares a year, he would gradually cover every farm and every country house in the home counties.

But obviously there was a bit more to it than that. Country folk are a suspicious lot. So are the impoverished rich. You can't go about ringing their bells and expecting them to show you around their houses just for the asking, because they won't do it. That way you would never get beyond the front door. How then was he to gain admittance? Perhaps it would be best if he didn't let them know he was a dealer at all. He could be the telephone man, the plumber, the gas inspector. He could even be a clergyman …

TR. 04

Von nun an war er jeden Sonntag ein netter alter Pfarrer, der seinen Feiertag opferte, um der «Gesellschaft» einen Liebesdienst zu erweisen, indem er ein Inventar der in englischen Bauernhöfen und Landhäusern verborgenen Schätze aufnahm. Und wer in aller Welt hätte gewagt, ihn hinauszuwerfen, wenn er das hörte?

Niemand.

War Mr. Boggis erst einmal drinnen und entdeckte zufällig etwas, was er gern haben wollte – nun, dann gab es hundert verschiedene Wege, zum Ziel zu kommen.

Zu seiner eigenen Überraschung ging alles wie am Schnürchen. Die Freundlichkeit, mit der er in einem Haus nach dem anderen empfangen wurde, war ihm anfangs sogar geradezu peinlich. Etwas kalte Pastete, ein Glas Portwein, eine Tasse Tee, einen Korb Pflaumen, ein reichhaltiges Sonntagsmahl im Kreise der Familie, dergleichen wurde ihm immer wieder angeboten, ja aufgedrängt. Mitunter waren natürlich auch Minuten der Angst und unangenehme Zwischenfälle zu verzeichnen, aber neun Jahre, das sind mehr als vierhundert Sonntage, und in diesem Zeitraum kann man sehr viele Häuser besuchen. Alles in allem war es ein interessantes, aufregendes und lukratives Geschäft.

Und nun war wieder Sonntag, und Mr. Boggis betätigte sich in der Grafschaft Buckinghamshire, in einem der nördlichsten Quadrate seiner Karte, ungefähr zehn Meilen von Oxford entfernt. Als er den Hügel hinabfuhr und sein erstes Haus, das verfallene im Queen-Anne-Stil, ansteuerte, stieg in ihm das Gefühl auf, dieser Tag werde sich zu einem seiner glücklichsten entwickeln.

Er parkte den Wagen in einigem Abstand vom Eingang und machte sich daran, die restlichen zweihundert Schritte zu Fuß zu gehen. Seinen Wagen ließ er nicht gern sehen, bevor ein Handel abgeschlossen war. Ein lieber alter Geistlicher und ein großer Kombiwagen schienen nicht recht zueinander zu passen. Der kurze Weg gab ihm zudem Gelegenheit, das Haus von außen zu betrachten und sich in eine der Situation entsprechende Stimmung zu versetzen.

From this point on, the whole scheme began to take on a more practical aspect. Mr Boggis ordered a large quantity of superior cards on which the following legend was engraved:

THE REVEREND
CYRIL WINNINGTON BOGGIS

President of the Society	*In association with*
for the Preservation of	*The Victoria and*
Rare Furniture	*Albert Museum*

From now on, every Sunday, he was going to be a nice old parson spending his holiday travelling around on a labour of love for the 'Society', compiling an inventory of the treasures that lay hidden in the country homes of England. And who in the world was going to kick him out when they heard that one?

Nobody.

And then, once he was inside, if he happened to spot something he really wanted, well – he knew a hundred different ways of dealing with that.

Rather to Mr Boggis's surprise, the scheme worked. In fact, the friendliness with which he was received in one house after another through the countryside was, in the beginning, quite embarrassing, even to him. A slice of cold pie, a glass of port, a cup of tea, a basket of plums, even a full sit-down Sunday dinner with the family, such things were constantly being pressed upon him. Sooner or later, of course, there had been some bad moments and a number of unpleasant incidents, but then nine years is more than four hundred Sundays, and that adds up to a great quantity of houses visited. All in all, it had been an interesting, exciting, and lucrative business.

And now it was another Sunday and Mr Boggis was operating in the county of Buckinghamshire, in one of the most northerly squares on his map, about ten miles from Oxford, and as he drove down the hill and headed for his first house, the dilapidated Queen Anne, he began to get the feeling that this was going to be one of his lucky days.

TR. 05

He parked the car about a hundred yards from the gates and got out to walk the rest of the way. He never liked people to see his car until after a deal was completed. A dear old clergyman and a large station-wagon somehow never seemed quite right together. Also the short walk gave him time to examine the property closely from the outside and to assume the mood most likely to be suitable for the occasion.

Mr. Boggis ging schnell die Auffahrt hinauf. Er war ein kleiner Mann, dickbäuchig, mit fleischigen Schenkeln und einem runden rosigen Gesicht, das wie gemacht für seine Rolle war. Die großen braunen Augen, die aus diesem rosigen Antlitz hervorquollen, wirkten ebenso freundlich wie dumm. Er war schwarz gekleidet, trug das übliche «Hundehalsband» der Geistlichen, und auf seinem Kopf saß ein weicher schwarzer Hut. In der Hand hielt er einen alten Spazierstock aus Eichenholz, der ihm seiner Meinung nach ein ländlich-gemütliches Aussehen verlieh.

Er näherte sich der Haustür und läutete. Gleich darauf hörte er Schritte in der Halle, die Tür öffnete sich, und vor ihm – oder eigentlich über ihm – stand eine riesenhaft große Frau in Reithosen. Nicht einmal der Rauch ihrer Zigarette konnte den kräftigen Geruch nach Stall und Pferdemist übertäuben, der von ihr ausging.

«Ja?» fragte sie mit einem mißtrauischen Blick. «Was wünschen Sie?»

Mr. Boggis, der halb und halb darauf gefaßt war, sie im nächsten Moment wiehern zu hören, lüftete den Hut, machte eine kleine Verbeugung, überreichte seine Karte und murmelte: «Entschuldigen Sie vielmals, daß ich Sie störe.» Dann wartete er und beobachtete ihr Gesicht, während sie las.

«Das verstehe ich nicht», sagte sie und gab ihm die Karte zurück. «Was wünschen Sie?»

Mr. Boggis erklärte ihr Zweck und Ziel der Gesellschaft zur Erhaltung seltenen Mobiliars.

Ihre Augen unter den hellen, buschigen Brauen starrten ihn grimmig an. «Hat das etwas mit der Sozialistischen Partei zu tun?» erkundigte sie sich.

Nun war es leicht. Mit einem Tory in Reithosen, ob männlich oder weiblich, kam Mr. Boggis immer gut zurecht. Er verwendete zwei Minuten auf ein begeistertes Lob des äußersten rechten Flügels der Konservativen und zwei weitere auf eine heftige Kritik an den Sozialisten. Als letzten Triumph spielte er die Tatsache aus, daß die Sozialisten einmal einen Gesetzentwurf für das Verbot der Parforcejagden auf dem Lande eingebracht hatten, und ging dann dazu über, der Dame seine Auffassung vom Himmel vorzutragen – «obwohl Sie das lieber nicht dem Bischof erzählen sollten». Für ihn, so sagte er, sei der Himmel ein Ort, wo man Füchse, Hirsche und Hasen mit großen Meuten unermüdlicher Hunde jagen könne, und zwar täglich, auch sonntags, vom Morgen bis zum Abend.

Er beobachtete sie, während er sprach, und bald sah er, daß der Zauber zu wirken begann. Die Lippen seiner Zuhörerin verzogen sich zu einem breiten Lächeln und entblößten dabei zwei Reihen riesiger gelblicher Zähne. «Madam», rief Mr. Boggis, «ich bitte Sie inständig, halten Sie mich bloß nicht für einen Sozialisten!»

Mr Boggis strode briskly up the drive. He was a small fat-legged man with a belly. The face was round and rosy, quite perfect for the part, and the two large brown eyes that bulged out at you from this rosy face gave an impression of gentle imbecility. He was dressed in a black suit with the usual parson's dog-collar round his neck, and on his head a soft black hat. He carried an old oak walking-stick which lent him, in his opinion, a rather rustic easy-going air.

He approached the front door and rang the bell. He heard the sound of foot-steps in the hall and the door opened and suddenly there stood before him, or rather above him, a gigantic woman dressed in riding-breeches. Even through the smoke of her cigarette he could smell the powerful odour of stables and horse manure that clung about her.

'Yes?' she asked, looking at him suspiciously. 'What is it you want?'

Mr Boggis, who half expected her to whinny any moment, raised his hat, made a little bow, and handed her his card. 'I do apologize for bothering you,' he said, and then he waited, watching her face as she read the message.

'I don't understand,' she said, handing back the card. 'What is it you want?'

Mr Boggis explained about the Society for the Preservation Rare Furniture.

'This wouldn't by any chance be something to do with the Socialist Party?' she asked, staring at him fiercely from under a pair of pale bushy brows.

From then on, it was easy. A Tory in riding-breeches, male or female, was always a sitting duck for Mr Boggis. He spent two minutes delivering an impassioned eulogy on the extreme Right Wing of the Conservative Party, then two more denouncing the Socialists. As a clincher, he made particular reference to the Bill that the Socialists had once introduced for the abolition of blood-sports in the country, and went on to inform his listener that his idea of heaven – 'though you better not tell the bishop, my dear' – was a place where one could hunt the fox, the stag, and the hare with large packs of tireless hounds from morn till night every day of the week, including Sundays.

Watching her as he spoke, he could see the magic beginning to do its work. The woman was grinning now, showing Mr Boggis a set of enormous, slightly yellow teeth. 'Madam,' he cried, 'I beg of you, *please* don't get me started on Socialism.' At that point, she let out a great guffaw of laughter, raised an enormous red hand, and slapped him so hard on the shoulder that he nearly went over.

'Come in!' she shouted. 'I don't know what the hell you want, but come on in!'

In diesem Augenblick brach sie in ein wieherndes Lachen aus, hob eine breite rote Hand und schlug ihm so kräftig auf die Schulter, daß er fast umgefallen wäre.

«Kommen Sie rein!» schrie sie. «Ich weiß nicht, was Sie wollen, aber kommen Sie in drei Teufels Namen rein!»

Unglücklicherweise und ziemlich überraschend gab es in diesem Hause nichts, was irgendwelchen Wert gehabt hätte, und Mr. Boggis, der an unfruchtbares Gebiet prinzipiell keine Zeit verschwendete, entschuldigte sich bald und ging. Der Besuch hatte kaum fünfzehn Minuten gedauert, und das, so sagte er sich, als er in seinen Wagen stieg, war genau das übliche für solche Fälle.

Nun hatte er nur noch Bauernhäuser zu besuchen, und das nächste lag ungefähr eine halbe Meile entfernt. Es war ein großes Fachwerkgebäude von beträchtlichem Alter, und seine Südwand wurde von einem prächtig blühenden Birnbaum verdeckt.

Mr. Boggis klopfte an die Tür. Er wartete, bekam aber keine Antwort und klopfte daher noch einmal. Als sich wieder nichts rührte, ging er um das Haus herum, denn er nahm an, der Bauer sei im Kuhstall. Auch auf dem Hof fand er niemanden. Sie werden wohl alle in der Kirche sein, dachte er und fing an, in die Fenster zu spähen, ob er etwas Interessantes entdecken könnte. Im Eßzimmer war nichts. Er versuchte es mit dem Wohnzimmer, und dort, direkt vor seiner Nase, erblickte er in der Fensternische ein wunderschönes Stück, einen halbrunden Spieltisch aus Mahagoni, reich mit Intarsien versehen, im Stil von Hepplewhite, um 1780.

«Aha!» sagte er laut und preßte das Gesicht gegen die Scheibe. «Gut gemacht, Boggis.»

Aber das war noch nicht alles. Da stand auch ein Stuhl, ein einzelner Stuhl, allem Anschein nach von noch besserer Qualität als der Tisch. Ebenfalls Hepplewhite, nicht wahr? Und so schön! Die Stäbe der Rückenlehne waren mit fein geschnitzten Blättern und Ranken verziert, das Rohrgeflecht des Sitzes war zweifellos echt, und was die anmutig geschweiften Beine betraf, so hatten die beiden hinteren jenen besonderen Schwung nach außen, der so viel bedeutet. Ein erlesener Stuhl. «Bevor dieser Tag vorüber ist», sagte Mr. Boggis ruhig vor sich hin, «werde ich die Freude haben, auf diesem entzückenden Stuhl zu sitzen.» Nie kaufte er einen Stuhl, ohne das zu tun. Für ihn war das die Probe aufs Exempel, und es war immer interessant zu sehen, wie er sich behutsam auf den Sitz sinken ließ und dabei auf das Nachgeben achtete, das ihm, dem Fachmann, genau verriet, wieweit die Jahre die Fugen und die Schwalbenschwanzverbindungen hatten eintrocknen lassen.

Es eilt nicht, sagte er sich und beschloß, später wiederzukommen. Er hatte ja den ganzen Nachmittag vor sich.

Unfortunately, and rather surprisingly, there was nothing of any value in the whole house, and Mr Boggis, who never wasted time on barren territory, soon made his excuses and took his leave. The whole visit had taken less than fifteen minutes, and that, he told himself as he climbed back into his car and started off for the next place, was exactly as it should be.

From now on, it was all farmhouses, and the nearest was about half a mile up the road. It was a large half-timbered brick building of considerable age, and there was a magnificent pear tree still in blossom covering almost the whole of the south wall.

TR. 06

Mr Boggis knocked on the door. He waited, but no one came. He knocked again, but still there was no answer, so he wandered around the back to look for the farmer among the cowsheds. There was no one there either. He guessed that they must all still be in church, so he began peering in the windows to see if he could spot anything interesting. There was nothing in the dining-room. Nothing in the library either. He tried the next window, the living-room, and there, right under his nose, in the little alcove that the window made, he saw a beautiful thing, a semicircular card-table in mahogany, richly veneered, and in the style of Hepplewhite, built around 1780.

'Ah-ha,' he said aloud, pressing his face hard against the glass. 'Well done, Boggis.'

But that was not all. There was a chair there as well, a single chair, and if he were not mistaken it was of an even finer quality than the table. Another Hepplewhite, wasn't it? And oh, what a beauty! The lattices on the back were finely carved with the honeysuckle, the husk, and the paterae, the caning on the seat was original, the legs were very gracefully turned and the two back ones had that peculiar outward splay that meant so much. It was an exquisite chair. 'Before this day is done,' Mr Boggis said softly, 'I shall have the pleasure of sitting down upon that lovely seat.' He never bought a chair without doing this. It was a favourite test of his, and it was always an intriguing sight to see him lowering himself delicately into the seat, waiting for the 'give', expertly gauging the precise but infinitesimal degree of shrinkage that the years had caused in the mortice and dovetail joints.

But there was no hurry, he told himself. He would return here later. He had the whole afternoon before him.

The next farm was situated some way back in the fields, and in order to keep his car out of sight, Mr Boggis had to leave it on the road and walk about

TR. 07

Der nächste Hof lag inmitten von Feldern. Damit man den Wagen nicht sah, mußte Mr. Boggis ihn auf der Landstraße stehenlassen und etwa sechshundert Schritte auf einem Seitenweg gehen, der in den hinteren Hof des Bauernhauses mündete. Wie er beim Näherkommen bemerkte, war dieses Anwesen erheblich kleiner als das vorige, so daß hier nicht viel zu erhoffen war. Alles sah vernachlässigt aus, und einige Ställe waren baufällig.

In einer Ecke des Hofes standen dicht beieinander drei Männer. Einer von ihnen hielt zwei große schwarze Windhunde an der Leine. Als die Männer den schwarzgekleideten Mr. Boggis mit seinem Pfarrerkragen herankommen sahen, verstummten sie, schienen plötzlich starr und steif zu werden und wandten ihm ihre Gesichter zu, um ihn argwöhnisch zu beäugen.

Der älteste von den dreien, ein untersetzter Mann mit breitem Froschmund und kleinen, verschmitzten Augen, hieß – was Mr. Boggis natürlich nicht wußte – Rummins und war der Besitzer des Hofes.

Der hochgewachsene junge Mann neben ihm, dessen eines Auge nicht ganz in Ordnung zu sein schien, war sein Sohn Bert.

Der kleine Mann mit dem flachen Gesicht, der niedrigen, faltigen Stirn und den ungeheuer breiten Schultern hieß Claud und hatte sich bei Rummins eingefunden, weil er ein Stück Schweinefleisch oder Schinken von dem tags zuvor geschlachteten Schwein zu ergattern hoffte. Claud wußte von der Schlachtung – das Quieken des Tieres war weithin zu hören gewesen –, und er wußte auch, daß man für so etwas eine behördliche Genehmigung brauchte, daß Rummins aber keine hatte.

«Guten Tag», sagte Mr. Boggis. «Schönes Wetter heute.»

Keiner der Männer rührte sich. Alle drei dachten genau dasselbe – daß dieser Geistliche, der ganz gewiß nicht aus der Gegend stammte, ein Abgesandter der Behörde sei und hier herumschnüffeln wolle.

«Was für schöne Hunde», fuhr Mr. Boggis fort. «Ich muß zwar gestehen, daß ich noch nie bei einem Windhundrennen war, aber es soll ja ein hochinteressanter Sport sein.»

Beharrliches Schweigen. Mr. Boggis blickte rasch von Rummins zu Bert, dann auf Claud und wieder auf Rummins, und stellte fest, daß sie alle den gleichen Gesichtsausdruck hatten, eine eigenartige Mischung von Spott und Herausforderung, mit einem geringschätzigen Kräuseln um den Mund und einem höhnischen Zug um die Nase.

«Darf ich fragen, ob Sie der Hofbesitzer sind?» wandte sich Mr. Boggis unerschrocken an Rummins.

«Was wünschen Sie?»

six hundred yards along a straight track that led directly into the back yard of the farmhouse. This place, he noticed as he approached, was a good deal smaller than the last, and he didn't hold out much hope for it. It looked rambling and dirty, and some of the sheds were clearly in bad repair.

There were three men standing in a close group in a corner of the yard, and one of them had two large black greyhounds with him, on leashes. When the men caught sight of Mr Boggis walking forward in his black suit and parson's collar, they stopped talking and seemed suddenly to stiffen and freeze, becoming absolutely still, motionless, three faces turned towards him, watching him suspiciously as he approached.

The oldest of the three was a stumpy man with a wide frog-mouth and small shifty eyes, and although Mr Boggis didn't know it, his name was Rummins and he was the owner of the farm.

The tall youth beside him, who appeared to have something wrong with one eye, was Bert, the son of Rummins.

The shortish flat-faced man with a narrow corrugated brow and immensely broad shoulders was Claud. Claud had dropped in on Rummins in the hope of getting a piece of pork or ham out of him from the pig that had been killed the day before. Claud knew about the killing – the noise of it had carried far across the fields – and he also knew that a man should have a government permit to do that sort of thing, and that Rummins didn't have one.

'Good afternoon,' Mr Boggis said. 'Isn't it a lovely day?'

None of the three men moved. At that moment they were all thinking precisely the same thing – that somehow or other this clergyman, who was certainly not the local fellow, had been sent to poke his nose into their business and to report what he found to the government.

'What beautiful dogs,' Mr Boggis said. 'I must say I've never been greyhound-racing myself, but they tell me it's a fascinating sport.'

Again the silence, and Mr Boggis glanced quickly from Rummins to Bert, then to Claud, then back again to Rummins, and he noticed that each of them had the same peculiar expression on his face, something between a jeer and a challenge, with a contemptuous curl to the mouth and a sneer around the nose.

'Might I inquire if you are the owner?' Mr Boggis asked, undaunted, addressing himself to Rummins.

'What is it you want?'

«Entschuldigen Sie vielmals, daß ich Sie störe, noch dazu an einem Sonntag.»

Mr. Boggis überreichte seine Karte, die Rummins nahm und dicht vor die Augen hielt. Die beiden anderen rührten sich nicht, schielten aber zur Seite und versuchten mitzulesen.

«Ja, was wollen Sie eigentlich?» fragte Rummins.

Zum zweiten Mal an diesem Tage erklärte Mr. Boggis umständlich Zweck und Ziel der Gesellschaft zur Erhaltung seltenen Mobiliars.

«So was haben wir nicht», knurrte Rummins, als der Vortrag beendet war. «Sie vergeuden nur Ihre Zeit.»

«Nicht so hastig, Sir», erwiderte Mr. Boggis mit erhobenem Finger. «Der letzte Mann, der mir das gesagt hat, war ein alter Bauer unten in Sussex, und als er mich schließlich doch ins Haus ließ, wissen Sie, was ich da in der Küchenecke gefunden habe? Einen schmutzigen alten Stuhl, der bei näherer Betrachtung *vierhundert Pfund* wert war! Ich habe dem Mann geholfen, ihn zu verkaufen, und er hat sich für das Geld einen Traktor angeschafft.»

«Was schwatzen Sie denn da?» sagte Claud. «Einen Stuhl, der vierhundert Pfund wert ist, gibt's auf der ganzen Welt nicht.»

«Entschuldigen Sie», antwortete Mr. Boggis steif, «aber ich kenne viele Stühle in England, die mehr als das Doppelte dieser Summe wert sind. Und wo befinden sie sich? Überall auf dem Lande sind sie auf Bauernhöfen und in Landhäusern versteckt und werden als Tritte oder Leitern benutzt. Tatsächlich, die Leute trampeln mit Nagelschuhen darauf herum, wenn sie einen Topf Marmelade vom Küchenschrank nehmen oder ein Bild aufhängen wollen. Ich sage Ihnen nur die Wahrheit, liebe Freunde.»

Rummins trat unbehaglich von einem Fuß auf den anderen.

«Sie meinen also, Sie wollen nur hineingehen, mitten im Zimmer stehenbleiben und sich umsehen?»

«Genau das», versicherte Mr. Boggis, dem allmählich klar wurde, wo hier der Hase im Pfeffer lag. «Ich will meine Nase weder in Ihre Schränke noch in Ihre Speisekammer stecken. Nur die Möbel möchte ich anschauen, um festzustellen, ob Sie zufällig irgend etwas Kostbares besitzen, über das ich in der Zeitschrift unserer Gesellschaft berichten könnte.»

«Wissen Sie, was ich glaube?» Rummins fixierte ihn mit seinen kleinen, boshaften Augen. «Ich glaube, Sie sind darauf aus, die Möbel auf eigene Rechnung zu kaufen. Wozu sollten Sie sich sonst soviel Mühe machen?»

«Ach, du lieber Himmel, ich wollte, ich hätte das Geld dazu. Natürlich, wenn ich etwas sehe, was mir gefällt, und es übersteigt meine Mittel nicht, dann komme ich

'I do apologize for troubling you, especially on a Sunday.'

Mr Boggis offered his card and Rummins took it and held it up close to his face. The other two didn't move, but their eyes swivelled over to one side, trying to see.

'And what exactly might you be wanting?' Rummins asked.

For the second time that morning, Mr Boggis explained at some length the aims and ideals of the Society for the Preservation of Rare Furniture.

'We don't have any,' Rummins told him when it was over. 'You're wasting your time.'

'Now, just a minute, sir,' Mr Boggis said, raising a finger. 'The last man who said that to me was an old farmer down in Sussex, and when he finally let me into his house, d'you know what I found? A dirty-looking old chair in the corner of the kitchen, and it turned out to be worth *four hundred pounds!* I showed him how to sell it, and he bought himself a new tractor with the money.'

'What on earth are you talking about?' Claud said. 'There ain't no chair in the world worth four hundred pound.'

'Excuse me,' Mr Boggis answered primly, 'but there are plenty of chairs in England worth more than twice that figure. And you know where they are? They're tucked away in the farms and cottages all over the country, with the owners using them as steps and ladders and standing on them with hobnailed boots to reach a pot of jam out of the top cupboard or to hang a picture. This is the truth I'm telling you, my friends.'

Rummins shifted uneasily on his feet.

'You mean to say all you want to do is go inside and stand there in the middle of the room and look around?'

'Exactly,' Mr Boggis said. He was at last beginning to sense what the trouble might be. 'I don't want to pry into your cupboards or into your larder. I just want to look at the furniture to see if you happen to have any treasures here, and then I can write about them in our Society magazine.'

'You know what I think?' Rummins said, fixing him with his small wicked eyes. 'I think you're after buying the stuff yourself. Why else would you be going to all this trouble?'

'Oh, dear me. I only wish I had the money. Of course, if I saw something that I took a great fancy to, and it wasn't beyond my means, I might be tempted to make an offer. But alas, that rarerely happens.'

'Well,' Rummins said, 'I don't suppose there's any harm in your taking a look around if that's all you want.' He led the way across the yard to the back door

schon mal in Versuchung, ein Angebot zu machen. Aber so was gibt's leider selten.»

«Schön», meinte Rummins, «wenn Sie weiter nichts wollen als sich umsehen, dann können Sie das meinetwegen tun.» Damit ging er über den Hof zur Hinterseite des Hauses, und Mr. Boggis folgte ihm. Auch Bert, der Sohn, und Claud mit seinen beiden Hunden schlossen sich an. Sie durchquerten die Küche – das einzige Möbelstück war dort ein billiger Tisch aus Tannenholz, auf dem ein totes Huhn lag – und traten in ein ziemlich großes, außerordentlich schmutziges Wohnzimmer.

Und da war sie! Mr. Boggis sah sie sofort, blieb wie angewurzelt stehen und schnappte hörbar nach Luft. Fünf, zehn, fünfzehn Sekunden, wenn nicht länger, stand er unbeweglich da und glotzte wie ein Idiot, weil er nicht zu glauben vermochte, nicht zu glauben wagte, daß er wirklich das sah, was er sah. Das *konnte* nicht wahr sein, unmöglich! Doch je länger er hinstarrte, desto wahrer schien es zu werden.

Ja, da war sie, unmittelbar vor ihm an der Wand, ebenso wirklich wie das Haus selbst! Und wer in der Welt hätte sich bei so einem Ding täuschen können? Zugegeben, sie war weiß angestrichen, aber das hatte nichts, gar nichts zu sagen. Irgendein Idiot hatte sie so verschandelt, und die Farbe war leicht zu entfernen. Du guter Gott! Was für eine Pracht! Und an so einem Ort!

In diesem Augenblick wurde sich Mr. Boggis bewußt, daß die drei Männer, Rummins, Bert und Claud, am Kamin lehnten und ihn scharf beobachteten. Sie hatten ihn stehenbleiben, nach Luft schnappen und glotzen sehen, sie mußten bemerkt haben, daß sein Gesicht rot – vielleicht auch blaß – geworden war, und wenn er nicht sofort etwas dagegen tat, würden sie ihm auf jeden Fall das Geschäft gründlich verderben. Rasch entschlossen, griff sich Mr. Boggis ans Herz, taumelte zum nächsten Stuhl und sank schwer atmend darauf nieder.

«Was haben Sie denn?» fragte Claud.

«Nichts», hauchte er. «Es geht gleich vorüber. Bitte – Wasser. Mein Herz …»

Bert holte ein Glas Wasser, gab es Mr. Boggis und blieb, ihn blöde anstarrend, neben ihm stehen.

«Ich dachte schon, Sie hätten was entdeckt», sagte Rummins. Sein schlaues Grinsen zog den Froschmund noch mehr in die Breite und enthüllte einige Zahnstummel.

«Nein, nein», beteuerte Mr. Boggis. «O nein, es ist nur mein Herz. Tut mir sehr leid, wirklich. Ich habe ab und zu so einen Anfall, aber das geht immer schnell vorüber. In ein paar Minuten bin ich wieder in Ordnung.»

Ich brauche Zeit zum Überlegen, dachte er. Vor allem aber muß ich mich ganz und gar fassen, bevor ich noch ein Wort sage. Reiß dich zusammen, Boggis. Was du auch tust, bleibe ruhig. Diese Leute mögen unwissend sein, aber dumm sind sie

of the farmhouse, and Mr Boggis followed him; so did the son Bert, and Claud with his two dogs. They went through the kitchen, where the only furniture was a cheap deal table with a dead chicken lying on it, and they emerged into a fairly large, exceedingly filthy living-room.

And there it was! Mr Boggis saw it at once, and he stopped dead in his tracks and gave a little shrill gasp of shock. Then he stood there for five, ten, fifteen seconds at least, staring like an idiot, unable to believe, not daring to believe what he saw before him. It *couldn't* be true, not possibly! But the longer he stared, the more true it began to seem. After all, there it was standing against the wall right in front of him, as real and as solid as the house itself. And who in the world could possibly make a mistake about a thing like that? Admittedly it was painted white, but that made not the slightest difference. Some idiot had done that. The paint could easily be stripped off. But good God! Just look at it! And in a place like this!

At this point, Mr Boggis became aware of the three men, Rummins, Bert, and Claud, standing together in a group over by the fireplace, watching him intently. They had seen him stop and gasp and stare, and they must have seen his face turning red, or maybe it was white, but in any event they had seen enough to spoil the whole goddamn business if he didn't do something about it quick. In a flash, Mr Boggis clapped one hand over his heart, staggered to the nearest chair, and collapsed into it, breathing heavily.

'What's the matter with you?' Claud asked.

'It's nothing,' he gasped. 'I'll be all right in a minute. Please – a glass of water. It's my heart.'

Bert fetched him the water, handed it to him, and stayed close beside him, staring down at him with a fatuous leer on his face.

'I thought maybe you were looking at something,' Rummins said. The wide frog-mouth widened a fraction further into a crafty grin, showing the stubs of several broken teeth.

'No, no,' Mr Boggis said. 'Oh dear me, no. It's just my heart. I'm so sorry. It happens every now and then. But it goes away quite quickly. I'll be all right in a couple of minutes.'

He *must* have time to think, he told himself. More important still, he must have time to compose himself thoroughly before he said another word. Take it gently, Boggis. And whatever you do, keep calm. These people may be ignorant, but they are not stupid. They are suspicious and wary and sly. And if it is really true – no it *can't* be, it *can't* be true …

nicht. Mißtrauisch sind sie, wachsam und gerissen. Und wenn es wirklich stimmt – nein, es *kann* nicht, kann nicht stimmen ...

Mit einer Gebärde des Schmerzes preßte er die Hand auf die Augen, öffnete sehr vorsichtig einen kleinen Spalt zwischen zwei Fingern und spähte hindurch.

Kein Zweifel, das Ding stand noch da, und er nahm die Gelegenheit wahr, es lange und gründlich zu betrachten. Ja, er hatte richtig gesehen, daran war nicht zu zweifeln. Es war einfach unglaublich.

Was er sah, war ein Möbel, für dessen Erwerb ein Fachmann so gut wie alles gegeben hätte. Einem Laien wäre es nicht weiter begehrenswert erschienen, zumal es mit schmutzigweißer Farbe bedeckt war, doch für Mr. Boggis war es der Wunschtraum eines Antiquitätenhändlers. Wie jeder Experte in Europa und Amerika wußte auch er, daß zu den bekanntesten und gesuchtesten Stücken englischer Möbelkunst des achtzehnten Jahrhunderts die berühmten «Chippendalekommoden» gehören. Er hätte ihre Geschichte im Schlaf hersagen können – die erste war 1920 in Moreton-in-Marsh entdeckt und in demselben Jahr bei Sotheby verkauft worden; die beiden anderen, die aus Raynham Hall, Norfolk, kamen, waren ein Jahr später aufgetaucht, ebenfalls in Sothebys Auktionsräumen. Alle drei hatten enorme Preise erzielt. An den genauen Preis der ersten und zweiten Kommode konnte sich Mr. Boggis nicht mehr erinnern, doch er wußte mit Sicherheit, daß die dritte dreitausendneunhundert Guineen eingebracht hatte. Und das im Jahre 1921! Heute war sie gewiß zehntausend Pfund wert. Irgend jemand – der Name des Mannes war Mr. Boggis entfallen – hatte vor nicht allzu langer Zeit eine Abhandlung über diese Kommoden geschrieben und einwandfrei nachgewiesen, daß alle drei aus derselben Werkstatt stammten. Wenn man auch keine Rechnungen gefunden hatte, so waren doch sämtliche Fachleute der Meinung, diese drei Kommoden könnte nur Thomas Chippendale selbst hergestellt haben, und zwar in seiner besten Zeit.

Und hier, sagte sich Mr. Boggis immer wieder, während er heimlich durch den Spalt zwischen seinen Fingern schaute, hier stand die vierte Chippendalekommode! Die *er* gefunden hatte! Reich würde er werden! Und berühmt! Jede der drei anderen war in der Welt der Kunsthändler unter einem besonderen Namen bekannt: die Chastletonkommode, die erste Raynhamkommode, die zweite Raynhamkommode. Diese würde als Boggiskommode in die Geschichte eingehen. Man brauchte sich nur die Gesichter der Leute in London vorzustellen, wenn sie den Fund morgen früh bewundern durften! Von den großen Händlern in West End – Frank Patridge, Mallett, Jetley und so weiter – würden phantastische Angebote einlaufen. Die *Times* würde ein Bild bringen und dazu schreiben: «Die Entdeckung dieser herrlichen Chippen-

He was holding one hand up over his eyes in a gesture of pain, and now, very carefully, secretly, he made a little crack between two of the fingers and peeked through.

Sure enough, the thing was still there, and on this occasion he took a good long look at it. Yes – he had been right the first time! There wasn't the slightest doubt about it! It was really unbelievable!

What he saw was a piece of furniture that any expert would have given almost anything to acquire. To a layman, it might not have appeared particularly impressive, especially when covered over as it was with dirty white paint, but to Mr Boggis it was a dealer's dream. He knew, as does every other dealer in Europe and America, that among the most celebrated and coveted examples of eighteenth-century English furniture in existence are the three famous pieces known as 'The Chippendale Commodes'. He knew their history backwards – that the first was 'discovered' in 1920, in a house at Moreton-in-Marsh, and was sold at Sotheby's the same year; that the other two turned up in the same auction rooms a year later, both coming out of Raynham Hall, Norfolk. They all fetched enormous prices. He couldn't quite remember the exact figure for the first one, or even the second, but he knew for certain that the last one to be sold had fetched thirty-nine hundred guineas. And that was in 1921! Today the same piece would surely be worth ten thousand pounds. Some man, Mr Boggis couldn't remember his name, had made a study of these commodes fairly recently and had proved that all three must have come from the same workshop, for the veneers were all from the same log, and the same set of templates had been used in the construction of each. No invoices had been found for any of them, but all the experts were agreed that these three commodes could have been executed only by Thomas Chippendale himself, with his own hands, at the most exalted period in his career.

And here, Mr Boggis kept telling himself as he peered cautiously through the crack in his fingers, here was the fourth Chippendale Commode! And *he* had found it! He would be rich! He would also be famous! Each of the other three was known throughout the furniture world by a special name – The Chastleton Commode, The First Raynham Commode, The Second Raynham Commode. This one would go down in history as The Boggis Commode! Just imagine the faces of the boys up there in London when they got a look at it tomorrow morning! And the luscious offers coming in from the big fellows over in the West End – Frank Partridge, Mallet, Jetley, and the rest of them! There would be a picture of it in *The Times*, and it would say, 'The very fine Chippen-

dalekommode verdanken wir dem Londoner Kunsthändler Mr. Cyril Boggis ...» Guter Gott, was für eine Aufregung das geben würde!

Diese hier, dachte Mr. Boggis, sieht genau aus wie die zweite Raynhamkommode. (Alle drei, die Chastleton und die beiden Raynhams, unterschieden sich durch allerlei Kleinigkeiten voneinander.) Es war ein höchst eindrucksvolles Möbelstück in französischem Rokokostil aus Chippendales Directoire-Periode, eine große, massige Kommode auf vier geschnitzten, ausgekehlten Beinen, die etwa einen Fuß hoch waren. Insgesamt hatte sie sechs Schubladen, zwei lange in der Mitte und zwei kürzere an jeder Seite. Die geschweifte Vorderpartie war oben, unten, links und rechts reich ornamentiert, und auch zwischen den mittleren und den seitlichen Schubladen sah man senkrecht verlaufende kunstvolle Schnitzereien in Form von Girlanden, Schnecken und Trauben. Die Messinggriffe waren zum Teil von dem weißen Anstrich überdeckt, schienen jedoch prächtig zu sein. Gewiß, die Kommode war ein ziemlich «schweres» Stück, aber so elegant, so graziös entworfen und ausgeführt, daß die Schwere nicht im geringsten störte.

«Wie fühlen Sie sich jetzt?» hörte Mr. Boggis jemanden fragen.

«Danke, danke, schon viel besser. Es geht immer schnell vorüber. Mein Doktor sagt, diese Anfälle seien ganz harmlos, ich müßte mich nur ein paar Minuten ruhig verhalten. Ach ja» – er erhob sich langsam –, «jetzt ist es besser.»

Vorsichtig, ein wenig schwankend, fing er an, im Zimmer umherzugehen und die Möbel einzeln zu begutachten. Er sah sofort, daß außer der Kommode nichts als Plunder vorhanden war.

«Hübscher Eichentisch», bemerkte er. «Nur fürchte ich, er ist nicht so alt, daß er irgendwie interessant wäre. Gute, bequeme Stühle, leider ganz modern, ja ganz modern. nd die Anrichte – nun, sie ist recht gefällig, aber ebenfalls ohne besonderen Wert. Diese Kommode» – er blieb vor der Chippendalekommode stehen und tippte geringschätzig mit dem Finger darauf –, «ein paar Pfund würden Sie vielleicht dafür kriegen, mehr gewiß nicht. Eine ziemlich plumpe Imitation. Vermutlich aus der Viktorianischen Zeit. Ist der weiße Anstrich von Ihnen?»

«Ja», antwortete Rummins. «Bert hat's gemacht.»

«Sehr vernünftig. In Weiß ist sie viel erträglicher.»

«Ein solides Stück», meinte Rummins. «Hat auch hübsche Schnitzereien.»

«Maschinenarbeit», erklärte Mr. Boggis in überlegenem Ton und bückte sich, um die meisterhafte Arbeit näher zu betrachten. «Das sieht man auf eine Meile. Immerhin, in seiner Art ist es ein nettes Stück. Hat seine Vorzüge.»

dale Commode which was recently discovered by Mr Cyril Boggis, a London dealer ... .' Dear God, what a stir he was going to make!

This one here, Mr Boggis thought, was almost exactly similar to the Second Raynham Commode. (All three, the Chastleton and the two Raynhams, differed from one another in a number of small ways.) It was a most impressive hand-some affair, built in the French rococo style of Chippendale's Directoire period, a kind of large fat chest-of-drawers set upon four carved and fluted legs that raised it about a foot from the ground. There were six drawers in all, two long ones in the middle and two shorter ones on either side. The serpentine front was magni-ficently ornamented along the top and sides and bottom, and also vertically between each set of drawers, with intricate carvings of festoons and scrolls and clusters. The brass handles, although partly obscured by white paint, appeared to be superb. It was, of course, a rather 'heavy' piece, but the design had been exe-cuted with such elegance and grace that the heaviness was in no way offensive.

'How're you feeling now?' Mr Boggis heard someone saying.

TR. 09

'Thank you, thank you, I'm much better already. It passes quickly. My doc-tor says it's nothing to worry about really so long as I rest for a few minutes whenever it happens. Ah yes,' he said, raising himself slowly to his feet. 'That's better. I'm all right now.'

A trifle unsteadily, he began to move around the room examining the furni-ture, one piece at a time, commenting upon it briefly. He could see at once that apart from the commode it was a very poor lot.

'Nice oak table,' he said. 'But I'm afraid it's not old enough to be of any in-terest. Good comfortable chairs, but quite modern, yes, quite modern. Now this cupboard, well, it's rather attractive, but again, not valuable. This chest-of-drawers' – he walked casually past the Chippendale Commode and gave it a little contemptuous flip with his fingers – 'worth a few pounds, I dare say, but no more. A rather crude reproduction, I'm afraid. Probably made in Victorian times. Did you paint it white?'

'Yes,' Rummins said, 'Bert did it.'

'A very wise move. It's considerably less offensive in white.'

'That's a strong piece of furniture,' Rummins said. 'Some nice carving on it too.'

'Machine-carved,' Mr Boggis answered superbly, bending down to examine the exquisite craftsmanship. 'You can tell it a mile off. But still, I suppose it's quite pretty in its way. It has its points.'

Er schlenderte weiter, schien sich plötzlich zu besinnen, und kehrte langsam um. Mit gerunzelter Stirn, die Hand am Kinn, den Kopf zur Seite geneigt, stand er wie in Gedanken versunken da und schaute auf die Kommode.

«Wissen Sie was?» sagte er so beiläufig, daß er nicht einmal die Stimme hob. «Mir fällt gerade ein – solche Beine, wie diese Kommode sie hat, suche ich schon lange. In meinem Häuschen habe ich einen recht aparten Tisch, so ein niedriges Ding, wie es die Leute vors Sofa stellen, eine Art Kaffeetischchen, und an dem haben mir im Herbst, als ich umzog, die dummen Packer die Beine völlig ruiniert. Dabei hänge ich so sehr an dem Tischchen. Ich habe immer meine dicke Bibel darauf liegen und die Notizen für meine Predigten.» Er machte eine Pause und strich sich mit dem Finger über das Kinn. «Jetzt dachte ich eben daran, daß sich die Beine Ihrer Kommode sehr gut verwerten ließen. Ja, tatsächlich. Man könnte sie ohne weiteres abschneiden und an meinen Tisch leimen.» Er wandte sich um und sah die drei Männer unbeweglich dastehen. Drei Paar Augen beobachteten ihn mißtrauisch, drei verschiedene Augenpaare, aber alle gleich ungläubig: Rummins' Schweinsäuglein, Clauds große, träge Augen und Berts Augen, deren eines sehr seltsam aussah, blaß, verschwommen, wie gesotten, mit einem kleinen schwarzen Punkt in der Mitte, wie ein Fischauge auf einem Teller.

Mr. Boggis schüttelte lächelnd den Kopf. «Ach, was rede ich denn da? Ich tue ja, als gehörte das Ding mir. Entschuldigen Sie.»

«Sie meinen, Sie wollen es kaufen?» fragte Rummins.

«Nun ...» Mr. Boggis warf einen Blick auf die Kommode und legte die Stirn in Falten. «Ich weiß nicht recht. Ich möchte schon ... und dann wieder ... wenn ich's mir überlege ... nein ... ich glaube, es würde doch zuviel Umstände machen. Das lohnt sich nicht. Ich lasse es lieber.»

«Wieviel würden Sie bieten?» erkundigte sich Rummins.

«Nicht viel, fürchte ich. Sehen Sie, es ist ja kein echtes altes Stück, bloß eine Nachahmung.»

«Das weiß man nicht so genau», widersprach Rummins. «Wir haben die Kommode seit über zwanzig Jahren im Haus, und vorher hat sie oben im Schloß gestanden. Dort habe ich sie auf der Auktion gekauft, als der alte Herr gestorben war. Neu ist das Ding also nicht, soviel steht fest.»

«Nicht gerade neu, aber bestimmt nicht älter als etwa sechzig Jahre.»

«O doch», beharrte Rummins. «Bert, wo ist der Zettel, den du mal hinten in einer Schublade gefunden hast? Die alte Rechnung.»

Der Sohn glotzte seinen Vater verständnislos an.

Mr. Boggis öffnete den Mund, schloß ihn aber sofort wieder, ohne einen Laut von

He began to saunter off, then he checked himself and turned slowly back again. He placed the tip of one finger against the point of his chin, laid his head over to one side, and frowned as though deep in thought.

'You know what?' he said, looking at the commode, speaking so casually that his voice kept trailing off. 'I've just remembered … I've been wanting a set of legs something like that for a long time. I've got a rather curious table in my own little home, one of those low things that people put in front of the sofa, sort of a coffee-table, and last Michaelmas, when I moved house, the foolish movers damaged the legs in the most shocking way. I'm very fond of that table. I always keep my big Bible on it, and all my sermon notes.'

He paused, stroking his chin with the finger. 'Now I was just thinking. These legs on your chest-of-drawers might be very suitable. Yes, they might indeed. They could easily be cut off and fixed on to my table.'

He looked around and saw the three men standing absolutely still, watching him suspiciously, three pairs of eyes, all different but equally mistrusting, small pig-eyes for Rummins, large slow eyes for Claud, and two odd eyes for Bert, one of them very queer and boiled and misty pale, with a little black dot in the centre, like a fish eye on a plate.

Mr Boggis smiled and shook his head. 'Come, come, what on earth am I saying? I'm talking as though I owned the piece myself. I do apologize.'

'What you mean to say is you'd like to buy it,' Rummins said.

'Well …' Mr Boggis glanced back at the commode, frowning. 'I'm not sure. I might … and then again … on second thoughts … no … I think it might be a bit too much trouble. It's not worth it. I'd better leave it.'

'How much were you thinking of offering?' Rummins asked.

'Not much, I'm afraid. You see, this is not a genuine antique. It's merely a reproduction.'

'I'm not so sure about that,' Rummins told him. 'It's been in *here* over twenty years, and before that it was up at the Manor House. I bought it there myself at auction when the old Squire died. You can't tell me that thing's new.'

'It's not exactly new, but it's certainly not more than about sixty years old.'

'It's more than that,' Rummins said. 'Bert, where's that bit of paper you once found at the back of one of them drawers? That old bill.'

The boy looked vacantly at his father.

Mr Boggis opened his mouth, then quickly shut it again without uttering a sound. He was beginning literally to shake with excitement, and to calm him-

sich zu geben. Er zitterte buchstäblich am ganzen Leibe. Um sich zu beruhigen, trat er ans Fenster und blickte auf den Hof, wo eine dicke braune Henne Körner aufpickte.

«Der Zettel lag hinten in einer Schublade unter den Kaninchenschlingen», sagte Rummins. «Los, hol ihn her und zeig ihn dem Pfarrer.»

Als Bert zur Kommode ging, drehte sich Mr. Boggis um. Er konnte nicht anders, er mußte ihm zuschauen. Der Bursche zog eine der mittleren Schubladen auf, und Mr. Boggis bemerkte, wie wundervoll weich sie herausglitt. Dann sah er Berts Hand unter Schnüren und Drähten herumwühlen.

«Meinst du das?» Bert brachte ein mehrmals geknifftes, gelbliches Blatt zum Vorschein und reichte es seinem Vater, der es entfaltete und dicht vor die Augen hielt.

«Wollen Sie mir etwa erzählen, daß dieses Schriftstück nicht steinalt ist?» Rummins hielt das Papier Mr. Boggis hin, der es mit zitternder Hand nahm. Es war spröde und knisterte leise zwischen den Fingern. Die Schrift war schräg, wie gestochen:

Edward Montagu, Esq.
schuldet dem Thos. Chippendale für eine große Mahagonny Kommode aus außerordentlich feinem Holze, sehr reich geschnitzet, auf ausgekehlten Beinen, zwey sehr hübsch geschweifte, lange Auszüge in der Mitten und zwey ditto an jeder Seite, mit reich ziselierten Messing Handgriffen und Ornamenten, alles in vollendetstem Geschmack ausgearbeitet f 87

Mr. Boggis hielt gewaltsam an sich, bemüht, die Erregung zu unterdrücken, die in seinem Innern wühlte und ihn schwindlig machte. O Gott, war das wundervoll! Mit dieser Nota stieg der Wert noch höher. Wieviel würde jetzt wohl herausspringen? Zwölf tausend Pfund? Vierzehn? Vielleicht fünfzehn oder gar zwanzig? Wer konnte das wissen?

Du lieber Himmel!

Geringschätzig ließ er das Papier auf den Tisch fallen und sagte kühl: «Na bitte, ich hab's ja gewußt – eine Viktorianische Nachahmung. Das hier ist einfach die Rechnung, die der Verkäufer – der Mann, der sie gemacht und für alt ausgegeben hat – seinem Kunden ausstellte. Von der Sorte habe ich schon viele gesehen. Beachten Sie, daß er nicht sagt, er hätte sie selbst angefertigt. Er war schlau genug, sich nicht zu verraten.»

«Sagen Sie, was Sie wollen», verkündete Rummins, «aber das ist ein altes Stück Papier.»

«Natürlich, mein lieber Freund. Es ist viktorianisch, spätviktorianisch. Etwa achtzehnhundertneunzig. Sechzig oder siebzig Jahre alt. Hunderte davon habe ich ge-

self he walked over to the window and stared out at a plump brown hen pecking around for stray grains of corn in the yard.

'It was in the back of that drawer underneath all them rabbit-snares,' Rummins was saying. 'Go on and fetch it out and show it to the parson.'

When Bert went forward to the commode, Mr Boggis turned round again. He couldn't stand not watching him. He saw him pull out one of the big middle drawers, and he noticed the beautiful way in which the drawer slid open. He saw Bert's hand dipping inside and rummaging around among a lot of wires and strings.

TR. 10

'You mean this?' Bert lifted out a piece of folded yellowing paper and carried it over to the father, who unfolded it and held it up close to his face.

'You can't tell me this writing ain't bloody old,' Rummins said, and he held the paper out to Mr Boggis, whose whole arm was shaking as he took it. It was brittle and it cracked slightly between his fingers. The writing was in a long sloping copperplate hand:

Edward Montagu, Esq.   Dr

To Thos. Chippendale

A large mahogany Commode Table of exceeding fine wood, very rich carvd, set upon fluted legs, two very neat shapd long drawers in the middle part and two ditto on each side, with rich chasd Brass Handles and Ornaments, the whole completely finished in the most exquisite taste £87

Mr Boggis was holding on to himself tight and fighting to suppress the excitement that was spinning round inside him and making him dizzy. Oh God, it was wonderful! With the invoice, the value had climbed even higher. What in heaven's name would it fetch now? Twelve thousand pounds? Fourteen? Maybe fifteen or even twenty? Who knows?

Oh, boy!

He tossed the paper contemptuously on to the table and said quietly, 'It's exactly what I told you, a Victorian reproduction. This is simply the invoice that the seller – the man who made it and passed it off as an antique – gave to his client. I've seen lots of them. You'll notice that he doesn't say he made it himself. That would give the game away.'

TR. 11

'Say what you like,' Rummins announced, 'but that's an old piece of paper.'

'Of course it is, my dear friend. It's Victorian, late Victorian. About eighteen ninety. Sixty or seventy years old. I've seen hundreds of them. That was a time

sehen. Damals gab es unzählige Tischler, die sich ein Gewerbe daraus machten, die schönen Möbel des achtzehnten Jahrhunderts zu imitieren.»

«Hören Sie, Herr Pfarrer ...» Rummins deutete mit einem dicken, schmutzigen Finger auf Mr. Boggis. «Ich sage ja nicht, daß Sie keine Ahnung von Möbeln haben, aber was ich sage, ist dies: Wie können Sie so mächtig sicher sein, daß die Kommode nachgemacht ist, wenn Sie gar nicht wissen, wie sie unter all der Farbe aussieht?»

«Kommen Sie», antwortete Mr. Boggis. «Kommen Sie her, ich will es Ihnen zeigen.» Er wartete, bis sich die anderen um ihn geschart hatten. «Hat jemand ein Messer?»

Claud förderte ein Taschenmesser mit Hornschale zutage. Mr. Boggis nahm es und öffnete die kleinste Klinge. Scheinbar nachlässig, in Wirklichkeit jedoch mit größter Vorsicht, begann er, oben auf der Kommode ein wenig Farbe abzukratzen. Die weiße Schicht blätterte von der harten, alten Politur sauber ab, und als er etwa drei Quadratzoll freigelegt hatte, trat er zurück und sagte: «So, nun schauen Sie sich das an.»

Es war wunderschön – ein kleiner Fleck Mahagoni, leuchtend wie ein Topas, warm und dunkel mit der echten Farbe seiner zweihundert Jahre.

«Na und?» fragte Rummins.

«Es ist behandelt. Das sieht doch jeder!»

«Wieso? Erklären Sie mal, woran man das sieht.»

«Schön. Ich muß allerdings sagen, daß so etwas nicht leicht zu erklären ist. Erfahrungssache, wissen Sie? Meine Erfahrung verrät mir ohne den leisesten Zweifel, daß dieses Holz mit Leim behandelt worden ist. Das geschieht, um dem Mahagoni die altersdunkle Farbe zu verleihen. Für Eiche nimmt man Pottasche und für Nußbaum Salpetersäure, aber für Mahagoni immer Leim.»

Die drei Männer kamen etwas näher, um das Holz zu betrachten. Die Sache fing offenbar an, sie zu interessieren. Von einer neuen Art Betrug oder Schwindel zu hören, ist immer spannend.

«Achten Sie auf die Maserung. Sehen Sie diese leichte Orangetönung in dem dunklen Rotbraun? Das ist das Zeichen von Leim.»

Sie beugten sich vor, die Nase dicht über dem Holz, zuerst Rummins, dann Claud, dann Bert.

«Und vor allem die Patina», fuhr Mr. Boggis fort.

«Die was?»

Er erklärte ihnen die Bedeutung des Wortes in Bezug auf Möbel.

«Sie haben keine Ahnung, liebe Freunde, wieviel Mühe sich diese Schufte machen, um die harte, schöne bronzefarbene Patina zu fälschen. Entsetzlich ist das, geradezu entsetzlich, und es macht mich ganz krank, davon zu reden.» Er spie jedes

when masses of cabinet-makers did nothing else but apply themselves to fak-ing the fine furniture of the century before.'

'Listen, Parson,' Rummins said, pointing at him with a thick dirty finger, 'I'm not saying as how you may not know a fair bit about this furniture business, but what I *am* saying is this: How on earth can you be so mighty sure it's a fake when you haven't even seen what it looks like underneath all that paint?'

'Come here,' Mr Boggis said. 'Come over here and I'll show you.' He stood beside the commode and waited for them to gather round. 'Now, anyone got a knife?'

Claud produced a horn-handled pocket knife, and Mr Boggis took it and opened the smallest blade. Then, working with apparent casualness but actu-ally with extreme care, he began chipping off the white paint from a small area on the top of the commode. The paint flaked away cleanly from the old hard varnish underneath, and when he had cleared away about three square inches, he stepped back and said, 'Now, take a look at that!'

It was beautiful – a warm little patch of mahogany, glowing like a topaz, rich and dark with the true colour of its two hundred years.

'What's wrong with it?' Rummins asked.

'It's processed! Anyone can see that!'

'How can you see it, Mister? You tell us.'

'Well, I must say that's a trifle difficult to explain. It's chiefly a matter of experience. My experience tells me that without the slightest doubt this wood has been processed with lime. That's what they use for mahogany, to give it that dark aged colour. For oak, they use potash salts, and for walnut it's nitric acid, but for mahogany it's always lime.'

The three men moved a little closer to peer at the wood. There was a slight stirring of interest among them now. It was always intriguing to hear about some new form of crookery or deception.

'Look closely at the grain. You see that touch of orange in among the dark red-brown. That's the sign of lime.'

They leaned forward, their noses close to the wood, first Rummins, then Claud, then Bert.

'And then there's the patina,' Mr Boggis continued.

'The what?'

He explained to them the meaning of this word as applied to furniture.

'My dear friends, you've no idea the trouble these rascals will go to to imi-

Wort von der Zungenspitze und verzog den Mund, um seinen Ekel zu zeigen.

Die Männer warteten, in der Hoffnung, weitere Geheimnisse zu erfahren.

«Wenn ich an die Zeit und Arbeit denke, die manche Sterbliche daran wenden, Unschuldige zu betrügen!» rief Mr. Boggis. «Einfach widerlich! Wissen Sie, meine Freunde, was hier geschehen ist? Ich kann es deutlich erkennen. Ja, ich sehe sie förmlich vor mir, diese Gauner, wie sie in einem langen, komplizierten Prozeß auf das mit Leinöl getränkte Holz entsprechend gefärbte französische Politur auftragen, die sie mit Bimsstein und Öl bürsten, mit einem Wachs einreiben, das voller Schmutz und Staub ist, und schließlich mit Hitze behandeln, damit die Politur springt und zweihundert Jahre alt aussieht! Wirklich, schon bei dem Gedanken an solche Schurkerei wird mir übel!»

Die drei Männer starrten unverwandt auf den kleinen dunklen Fleck.

«Fühlen Sie das Holz an!» befahl Mr. Boggis. «Legen Sie die Finger darauf! Na, wie kommt es Ihnen vor, warm oder kalt?»

«Kalt», sagte Rummins.

«Sehr richtig, mein Freund! Es ist eine bekannte Tatsache, daß sich gefälschte Patina immer kalt anfühlt. Bei echter hat man den Eindruck, sie sei warm.»

«Die hier fühlt sich ganz normal an», behauptete Rummins streitlustig.

«Nein, Sir, kalt. Aber natürlich braucht man Erfahrung und Fingerspitzengefühl, um ein endgültiges Urteil abgeben zu können. Von Ihnen darf man wirklich nicht erwarten, daß Sie mehr von Möbeln verstehen als ich beispielsweise von der Qualität Ihrer Gerste. Alles im Leben, mein lieber Freund, beruht auf Erfahrung.»

Die Männer starrten den merkwürdigen Geistlichen mit dem Mondgesicht und den hervorquellenden Augen nicht mehr ganz so mißtrauisch an, denn offenbar kannte er sich auf seinem Gebiet aus. Allerdings waren sie noch weit davon entfernt, ihm zu glauben.

Mr. Boggis bückte sich und wies auf einen der metallenen Handgriffe an der Kommode. «Das ist auch Fälscherarbeit», sagte er. «Altes Messing hat für gewöhnlich einen ganz charakteristischen Farbton. Wußten Sie das?»

Begierig, noch mehr Kniffe zu erfahren, blickten sie ihn an.

«Leider Gottes haben diese Schurken eine außerordentliche Geschicklichkeit erworben, besagten Farbton zu imitieren. Es ist praktisch unmöglich, zwischen ‹echtem altem› und ‹künstlichem altem› zu unterscheiden. Ich gebe offen zu, daß auch ich in diesem Punkt nur auf Vermutungen angewiesen bin. Es lohnt sich also nicht, die Farbe von den Handgriffen abzukratzen. Wir würden dadurch kein bißchen klüger werden.»

«Wie kann man denn neues Messing auf alt zurechtmachen?» erkundigte sich Claud. «Messing rostet doch nicht.»

tate the hard beautiful bronze-like appearance of genuine patina. It's terrible, really terrible, and it makes me quite sick to speak of it!' He was spitting each word sharply off the tip of the tongue and making a sour mouth to show his extreme distaste. The men waited, hoping for more secrets.

'The time and trouble that some mortals will go to in order to deceive the innocent!' Mr Boggis cried. 'It's perfectly disgusting! D'you know what they did here, my friends? I can recognize it clearly. I can almost *see* them doing it, the long, complicated ritual of rubbing the wood with linseed oil, coating it over with french polish that has been cunningly coloured, brushing it down with pumice-stone and oil, beeswaxing it with a wax that contains dirt and dust, and finally giving it the heat treatment to crack the polish so that it looks like two-hundred-year-old varnish! It really upsets me to contemplate such knavery!'

The three men continued to gaze at the little patch of dark wood.

'Feel it!' Mr Boggis ordered. Put your fingers on it! There, how does it feel, warm or cold?'

'Feels cold,' Rummins said.

'Exactly, my friend! It happens to be a fact that faked patina is always cold to the touch. Real patina has a curiously warm feel to it.'

'This feels normal,' Rummins said, ready to argue.

'No, sir, it's cold. But of course it takes an experienced and sensitive finger-tip to pass a positive judgement. You couldn't really be expected to judge this any more than I could be expected to judge the quality of your barley. Every-thing in life, my dear sir, is experience.'

The men were staring at this queer moon-faced clergyman with the bulging eyes, not quite so suspiciously now because he did seem to know a bit about his subject. But they were still a long way from trusting him.

Mr Boggis bent down and pointed to one of the metal drawer-handles on the commode. 'This is another place where the fakers go to work,' he said. 'Old brass normally has a colour and character all of its own. Did you know that?'

TR. 12

They stared at him, hoping for still more secrets.

'But the trouble is that they've become exceedingly skilled at matching it. In fact it's almost impossible to tell the difference between "genuine old" and "faked old". I don't mind admitting that it has me guessing. So there's not really any point in our scraping the paint off these handles. We wouldn't be any the wiser.'

'How can you possibly make new brass look like old?' Claud said. 'Brass doesn't rust, you know.'

«Stimmt genau, mein Freund, aber diese Verbrecher haben ihre geheimen Methoden.»

«Nämlich?» Claud ließ nicht locker. Seiner Meinung nach war jede Information dieser Art wertvoll. Man weiß ja nie, was die Zukunft bringt.

«Die Fälscher», dozierte Mr. Boggis, «brauchen nichts weiter zu tun, als die Handgriffe über Nacht in Mahagonispäne zu legen, die mit Salmiak getränkt sind. Der Salmiak färbt das Metall grün, aber wenn man das Grün abreibt, kommt darunter ein zarter silbriger Glanz zum Vorschein, genau der Glanz, den sehr altes Messing hat. Ach, auf was die alles verfallen! Für Eisen haben sie wieder einen anderen Trick.»

«Was tun sie mit Eisen?» fragte Claud interessiert.

«Mit Eisen ist die Sache sehr einfach», erklärte Mr. Boggis. «Eiserne Schlösser, Platten und Scharniere werden mit gewöhnlichem Salz bedeckt, und nach kurzer Zeit kann man sie verrostet und fleckig herausnehmen.»

«Schön», sagte Rummins, «Sie geben also zu, daß Sie über die Griffe nichts Genaues wissen. Mit anderen Worten, die Dinger können ohne weiteres viele hundert Jahre alt sein. Stimmt's?»

Mr. Boggis richtete seine hervorquellenden braunen Augen auf Rummins. «O nein», flüsterte er, «da irren Sie sich. Passen Sie auf.»

Er nahm aus seiner Jackentasche einen kleinen Schraubenzieher und gleichzeitig, ohne daß es jemand bemerkte, eine Messingschraube, die er in der Handfläche verbarg. Dann wählte er eine der Schrauben an der Kommode aus – an jedem Griff befanden sich vier – und befreite sie behutsam von der weißen Farbe, die ihr anhaftete. Als das erledigt war, drehte er sie langsam heraus.

«Wenn es eine echte Messingschraube aus dem achtzehnten Jahrhundert ist», sagte er, «dann wird das Gewinde etwas unregelmäßig sein, ein Zeichen, daß sie mit der Hand gefeilt worden ist. Haben wir es aber mit einer Fälschung aus der Viktorianischen Zeit oder später zu tun, so wird auch die Schraube jüngeren Datums sein und sich als maschinell hergestelltes Massenprodukt erweisen. Jeder kann so ein Serienfabrikat erkennen. Nun, wir werden sehen.»

Während Mr. Boggis die Hände über die alte Schraube legte und sie herauszog, gelang es ihm mühelos, sie mit der neuen zu vertauschen, die er zwischen zwei Fingern versteckt hielt. Das war ein Trick, der sich im Laufe der Jahre immer wieder von neuem bewährt hatte. In den Taschen seines geistlichen Rocks trug er stets eine Anzahl billiger Messingschrauben in den verschiedensten Größen mit sich herum.

«Na bitte», sagte er und reichte Rummins die moderne Schraube. «Überzeugen Sie sich selbst. Sehen Sie, wie gleichmäßig das Gewinde ist. Natürlich sehen Sie es.

'You are quite right, my friend. But these scoundrels have their own secret methods.'

'Such as what?' Claud asked. Any information of this nature was valuable, in his opinion. One never knew when it might come in handy.

'All they have to do,' Mr Boggis said, 'is to place these handles overnight in a box of mahogany shavings saturated in sal ammoniac. The sal ammoniac turns the metal green, but if you rub off the green, you will find underneath it a fine soft silvery-warm lustre, a lustre identical to that which comes with very old brass. Oh, it is so bestial, the things they do! With iron they have another trick.'

'What do they do with iron?' Claud asked, fascinated.

'Iron's easy,' Mr Boggis said. 'Iron locks and plates and hinges are simply buried in common salt and they come out all rusted and pitted in no time.'

'All right,' Rummins said. 'So you admit you can't tell about the handles. For all you know, they may be hundreds and hundreds of years old. Correct?'

'Ah,' Mr Boggis whispered, fixing Rummins with two big bulging brown eyes. 'That's where you're wrong. Watch this.'

From his jacket pocket, he took out a small screwdriver. At the same time, although none of them saw him do it, he also took out a little brass screw which he kept well hidden in the palm of his hand. Then he selected one of the screws in the commode – there were four to each handle – and began carefully scraping all traces of white paint from its head. When he had done this, he started slowly to unscrew it.

'If this is a genuine old brass screw from the eighteenth century,' he was saying, 'the spiral will be slightly uneven and you'll be able to see quite easily that it has been hand-cut with a file. But if this brasswork is faked from more recent times, Victorian or later, then obviously the screw will be of the same period. It will be a mass-produced, machine-made article. Anyone can recognize a machine-made screw. Well, we shall see.'

It was not difficult, as he put his hands over the old screw and drew it out, for Mr Boggis to substitute the new one hidden in his palm. This was another little trick of his, and through the years it had proved a most rewarding one. The pockets of his clergyman's jacket were always stocked with a quantity of cheap brass screws of various sizes.

'There you are,' he said, handing the modern screw to Rummins. 'Take a look at that. Notice the exact evenness of the spiral? See it? Of course you do. It's

Dies hier ist eine ganz gewöhnliche Schraube, wie sie in jeder Eisenwarenhandlung verkauft wird.»

Die Schraube ging von Hand zu Hand, und alle drei Männer betrachteten sie genau. Sogar Rummins zeigte sich beeindruckt.

Mr. Boggis steckte den Schraubenzieher in die Tasche und mit ihm die handgefertigte Schraube, die er aus der Kommode entfernt hatte. Dann machte er kehrt und schritt langsam an den drei Männern vorbei.

«Meine lieben Freunde», sagte er, als er die Tür zur Küche erreicht hatte, «es war sehr freundlich von Ihnen, daß Sie mir erlaubt haben, einen Blick in Ihr kleines Heim zu werfen, wirklich sehr freundlich. Ich hoffe nur, daß ich Sie nicht zu sehr belästigt habe.»

Rummins, der noch immer die Schraube untersuchte, blickte auf. «Sie haben nicht gesagt, wieviel Sie bieten», bemerkte er.

«Ach ja», antwortete Mr. Boggis, «da haben Sie recht. Wieviel ich biete? Nun, wenn ich ehrlich sein soll, ich finde, es lohnt sich nicht recht. Viel zu umständlich. Ich glaube, ich lasse es lieber.»

«Wieviel wollten Sie denn geben?»

«Möchten Sie die Kommode wirklich loswerden?»

«Daß ich sie loswerden möchte, habe ich nicht gesagt. Ich habe nur gefragt: wieviel.»

Mr. Boggis schaute auf die Kommode, neigte den Kopf erst auf die eine Seite, dann auf die andere, zog die Stirn kraus, schob die Lippen vor, zuckte die Achseln und machte eine kleine verächtliche Handbewegung, um anzudeuten, es lohne sich gar nicht, ernsthaft darüber zu reden.

«Sagen wir ... zehn Pfund. Ich meine, das wäre angemessen.»

«Zehn Pfund!» rief Rummins. «Seien Sie doch nicht komisch, Herr Pfarrer, *bitte!*»

«Als Brennholz wäre die Kommode schon teurer», erklärte Claud entrüstet.

«Schauen Sie sich die Rechnung an!» Rummins stach mit seinem schmutzigen Zeigefinger so heftig auf das kostbare Dokument ein, daß Mr. Boggis vor Angst verging. «Hier steht, was sie gekostet hat. Siebenundachtzig Pfund! Und da war sie neu. Jetzt ist sie antik und mindestens das Doppelte wert.»

«Entschuldigen Sie, Sir, so ist es nun doch nicht. Schließlich ist die Kommode eine Nachahmung. Aber ich will Ihnen was sagen, mein Freund – ich weiß, daß ich leichtsinnig bin, das liegt nun mal in meiner Natur –, ich werde Ihnen fünfzehn Pfund geben. Wie wär's?»

«Fünfzig», forderte Rummins.

just a cheap common little screw you yourself could buy today in any ironmonger's in the country.'

The screw was handed round from the one to the other, each examining it carefully. Even Rummins was impressed now.

Mr Boggis put the screwdriver back in his pocket together with the fine hand-cut screw that he'd taken from the commode, and then he turned and walked slowly past the three men towards the door.

'My dear friends,' he said, pausing at the entrance to the kitchen, 'it was so good of you to let me peep inside your little home – so kind. I do hope I haven't been a terrible old bore.'

Rummins glanced up from examining the screw. 'You didn't tell us what you were going to offer,' he said.

'Ah,' Mr Boggis said. 'That's quite right. I didn't, did I? Well, to tell you the honest truth, I think it's all a bit too much trouble. I think I'll leave it.'

'How much would you give?'

'You mean that you really wish to part with it?'

'I didn't say I wished to part with it. I asked you how much.'

Mr Boggis looked across at the commode, and he laid his head first to one side, then to the other, and he frowned, and pushed out his lips, and shrugged his shoulders, and gave a little scornful wave of the hand as though to say the thing was hardly worth thinking about really, was it?

'Shall we say ... ten pounds. I think that would be fair.'

'Ten pounds!' Rummins cried. 'Don't be so ridiculous, Parson, *please!*'

'It's worth more'n that for firewood!' Claud said, disgusted. 'Look here at the bill!' Rummins went on, stabbing that precious document so fiercely with his dirty fore-finger that Mr Boggis became alarmed. 'It tells you exactly what it cost! Eighty-seven pounds! And that's when it was new. Now it's antique it's worth double!'

'If you'll pardon me, no, sir, it's not. It's a second-hand reproduction. But I'll tell you what, my friend – I'm being rather reckless, I can't help it – I'll go up as high as fifteen pounds. How's that?'

'Make it fifty,' Rummins said.

A delicious little quiver like needles ran all the way down the back of Mr Boggis's legs and then under the soles of his feet. He had it now. It was his. No question about that. But the habit of buying cheap, as cheap as it was

Ein köstlicher kleiner Schauer, prickelnd wie Nadelstiche, lief über Mr. Boggis' Rücken und an den Beinen hinab bis unter die Fußsohlen. Er hatte sie. Jetzt war sie sein. Ohne jeden Zweifel. Aber billig kaufen, so billig wie menschenmöglich, war ihm unter dem Druck der Verhältnisse und durch jahrelange Übung so sehr zur Gewohnheit geworden, daß er es einfach nicht fertigbrachte, sofort zuzustimmen.

«Lieber Mann», flüsterte er sanft, «ich kann ja nur die Beine der Kommode gebrauchen. Vielleicht lassen sich später auch einmal die Schubladen verwerten, aber alles übrige, das Gestell selbst, ist nur Brennholz, wie Ihr Freund sehr richtig sagte.»

«Na, dann fünfunddreißig», schlug Rummins vor.

«Ich *kann* nicht, Sir, ich *kann* nicht! Soviel ist sie nicht wert. Überhaupt – ich weiß gar nicht, wie ich dazu komme, derart um einen Preis zu feilschen. Das schickt sich nicht für mich. Ich will Ihnen ein letztes Angebot machen: Zwanzig Pfund.»

«Einverstanden», rief Rummins hastig. «Sie gehört Ihnen.»

«Ach herrje», sagte Mr. Boggis und faltete die Hände. «Nun habe ich mich doch wieder verleiten lassen. Ich hätte das gar nicht tun dürfen.»

«Jetzt können Sie nicht mehr zurück, Herr Pfarrer. Verkauft ist verkauft.»

«Ja, ja, ich weiß.»

«Wie wollen Sie das Ding fortschaffen?»

«Hm ... Ich könnte meinen Wagen hier auf den Hof fahren, und wenn dann die Herren so freundlich wären, mir beim Verladen zu helfen ...»

«In einen Wagen? Das Ding paßt doch in keinen Wagen! Dazu brauchen Sie ein Auto mit Ladefläche.»

«Ach, ich glaube, es geht auch so. Wir wollen's jedenfalls probieren. Mein Wagen steht auf der Landstraße. Ich bin gleich zurück. Irgendwie schaffen wir das schon.»

Mr. Boggis ging über den Hof, durch das Tor und dann den langen Weg zur Straße hinunter. Er konnte ein leises Kichern nicht unterdrücken, und ihm war, als stiegen Hunderte und aber Hunderte kleiner Blasen, kribbelnd wie Selterswasser, aus seinem Magen auf und platzten vergnügt in seinem Kopf. Alle Butterblumen auf den Feldern hatten sich in Goldstücke verwandelt, die im Sonnenlicht blitzten. Der Boden war mit ihnen übersät, und Mr. Boggis wich vom Wege ab, damit er zwischen ihnen, auf ihnen gehen und den leisen metallischen Ton hören konnte, wenn er sie mit den Füßen zertrat. Kaum vermochte er sich so weit im Zaum zu halten, daß er nicht anfing zu rennen. Aber Geistliche rennen nie. Sie gehen schön gemächlich. Langsam, Boggis. Bleib ruhig, Boggis. Du hast keine Eile. Die Kommode gehört dir! Für zwanzig Pfund, und dabei ist sie fünfzehn- oder zwanzigtausend wert! Die Boggiskommode! In zehn Minuten wird sie in deinem Wagen stehen – das Verladen ist ja nicht weiter

humanly possible to buy, acquired by years of necessity and practice, was too strong in him now to permit him to give in so easily.

'My dear man,' he whispered softly, 'I only *want* the legs. Possibly I could find some use for the drawers later on, but the rest of it, the carcass itself, as your friend so rightly said, it's firewood, that's all.'

'Make it thirty-five,' Rummins said.

'I *couldn't* sir, I *couldn't!* It's not worth it. And I simply mustn't allow myself to haggle like this about a price. It's all wrong. I'll make you one final offer, and then I must go. Twenty pounds.'

'I'll take it,' Rummins snapped. 'It's yours.'

'Oh dear,' Mr Boggis said, clasping his hands. 'There I go again. I should never have started this in the first place.'

'You can't back out now, Parson. A deal's a deal.'

'Yes, yes, I know.'

'How're you going to take it?'

'Well, let me see. Perhaps if I were to drive my car up into the yard, you gentlemen would be kind enough to help me load it?'

'In a car? This thing'll never go in a car! You'll need a truck for this!'

'I don't think so. Anyway, we'll see. My car's on the road. I'll be back in a jiffy. We'll manage it somehow, I'm sure.'

Mr Boggis walked out into the yard and through the gate and then down the long track that led across the field towards the road. He found himself giggling quite uncontrollably, and there was a feeling inside him as though hundreds and hundreds of tiny bubbles were rising up from his stomach and bursting merrily in the top of his head, like sparkling-water. All the buttercups in the field were suddenly turning into golden sovereigns, glistening in the sunlight. The ground was littered with them, and he swung off the track on to the grass so that he could walk among them and tread on them and hear the little metallic tinkle they made as he kicked them around with his toes. He was finding it difficult to stop himself from breaking into a run. But clergymen never run; they walk slowly. Walk slowly, Boggis. Keep calm, Boggis. There's no hurry now. The commode is yours! Yours for twenty pounds, and it's worth fifteen or twenty thousand! The Boggis Commode! In ten minutes it'll be loaded into your car – it'll go in easily – and you'll be driving back to London and singing all the way! Mr Boggis driving the Boggis Commode home in the Boggis car. Historic oc-

schwierig –, du wirst nach London zurückfahren und unterwegs in einem fort singen! Boggis fährt die Boggiskommode in Boggis' Wagen heim. Ein historischer Augenblick. Was würde ein Reporter darum geben, könnte er dieses Ereignis im Bild festhalten! Ob man das arrangieren sollte? Vielleicht. Warten wir's ab. O du herrlicher Tag. Du köstlicher, sonniger Sommertag! Es ist eine Lust zu leben!

Auf dem Hof sagte unterdessen Rummins: «Stellt euch bloß vor, zwanzig Pfund gibt der alte Esel für solchen Plunder.»

«Gut haben Sie das gemacht, Mr. Rummins», lobte Claud.

«Glauben Sie, daß er zahlen wird?»

«Wir laden die Kommode nicht eher in den Wagen, bis er's getan hat.»

«Und wenn sie nun nicht hineingeht?» fragte Claud. «Wissen Sie, was ich denke, Mr. Rummins? Wollen Sie meine ehrliche Meinung hören? Ich denke, das verdammte Ding ist viel zu groß, als daß wir's je in den Wagen kriegen. Und was dann? Zum Teufel damit, wird er dann sagen und ohne die Kommode davonfahren. Auf Nimmerwiedersehen, mitsamt dem Geld. Sehr viel schien ihm ja an der Kommode gar nicht zu liegen.»

Rummins schwieg, um diese neue, ziemlich beunruhigende Möglichkeit zu erwägen.

«Wie soll denn so ein Ding in einen Wagen passen?» fuhr Claud unbarmherzig fort. «Geistliche haben nie große Wagen. Oder haben Sie schon mal einen Pfarrer mit einem großen Wagen gesehen, Mr. Rummins?»

«Nicht daß ich wüßte.»

«Na bitte. Und nun hören Sie zu. Mir ist da was eingefallen. Nicht wahr, er hat doch gesagt, er will nur die Beine? Stimmt's? Wir brauchen also nichts weiter zu tun, als sie hier abzusägen, bevor er zurückkommt, dann geht das Ding bestimmt in den Wagen. Und außerdem ersparen wir ihm damit viel Arbeit und Mühe. Was halten Sie davon?» Clauds flaches Rindsgesicht glänzte vor dummem Stolz.

«Keine schlechte Idee», sagte Rummins mit einem Blick auf die Kommode. «Eigentlich sogar eine verdammt gute Idee. Also dann los, wir müssen uns beeilen. Ihr beide tragt sie auf den Hof, und ich hole die Säge. Aber zieht zuerst die Schubladen raus.»

Wenige Minuten später hatten Claud und Bert die Kommode hinausgeschafft und sie mitten in dem Hühnerdreck und dem Kuhmist auf den Kopf gestellt. In der Ferne, auf halbem Wege zwischen Hof und Straße, sahen sie eine kleine schwarze Gestalt dahineilen. Sie schauten ihr nach. Die Gestalt benahm sich einigermaßen komisch. Von Zeit zu Zeit fiel sie in Trab, dann wieder hüpfte sie auf einem Bein oder vollführte Luftsprünge, und auf einmal schienen Töne eines lustigen Liedchens über die Wiese zu dringen.

casion. What *wouldn't* a newspaperman give to get a picture of that! Should he arrange it? Perhaps he should. Wait and see. Oh, glorious day! Oh, lovely sunny summer day! Oh, glory be!

Back in the farmhouse, Rummins was saying, 'Fancy that old bastard giving twenty pound for a load of junk like this.'

TR. 14

'You did very nicely, Mr Rummins,' Claud told him. 'You think he'll pay you?'

'We don't put it in the car till he do.'

'And what if it won't go in the car?' Claud asked. 'You know what I think, Mr Rummins? You want my honest opinion? I think the bloody thing's too big to go in the car. And then what happens? Then he's going to say to hell with it and just drive off without it and you'll never see him again. Nor the money either. He didn't seem all that keen on having it, you know.'

Rummins paused to consider this new and rather alarming prospect.

'How can a thing like that possibly go in a car?' Claud went on relentlessly. 'A parson never has a big car anyway. You ever seen a parson with a big car, Mr Rummins?'

'Can't say I have.'

'Exactly! And now listen to me. I've got an idea. He told us, didn't he, that it was only the legs he was wanting. Right? So all we've got to do is to cut 'em off quick right here on the spot before he comes back, then it'll be sure to go in the car. All we're doing is saving him the trouble of cutting them off himself when he gets home. How about it, Mr Rummins?' Claud's flat bovine face glimmered with a mawkish pride.

'It's not such a bad idea at that,' Rummins said, looking at the commode. 'In fact it's a bloody good idea. Come on then, we'll have to hurry. You and Bert carry it out into the yard. I'll get the saw. Take the drawers out first.'

Within a couple of minutes, Claud and Bert had carried the commode out-side and had laid it upside down in the yard amidst the chicken droppings and cow dung and mud. In the distance, half-way across the field, they could see a small black figure striding along the path towards the road. They paused to watch. There was something rather comical about the way in which this figure was conducting itself. Every now and again it would break into a trot, then it did a kind of hop, skip, and jump, and once it seemed as though the sound of a cheerful song came rippling faintly to them from across the meadow.

'I reckon he's balmy,' Claud said, and Bert grinned darkly, rolling his misty eye slowly round in its socket.

«Bei dem ist eine Schraube locker», meinte Claud lachend. Bert grinste vielsagend, und sein schlimmes Auge rollte langsam hin und her.

Rummins, plump wie ein Frosch, kam vom Schuppen herübergewatschelt. Claud nahm ihm die große Säge ab und machte sich ans Werk.

«Dicht absägen», sagte Rummins. «Sie wissen ja, er braucht sie für einen anderen Tisch.»

Das Mahagoniholz war hart und sehr trocken. Feiner roter Staub sprühte von dem Blatt der Säge und fiel sanft zu Boden.

Ein Bein nach dem anderen löste sich, und als alle abgesägt waren, bückte sich Bert und legte sie sorgsam in eine Reihe.

Claud trat zurück, um das Ergebnis seiner Arbeit zu betrachten. Eine längere Pause entstand.

«Nur eine Frage, Mr. Rummins», sagte er schließlich. «Auch so, wie es jetzt ist – könnten Sie dieses Ungetüm hinten in einen Wagen laden?»

«Müßte schon ein Kombiwagen sein.»

«Richtig!» rief Claud. «Aber Geistliche fahren keine Kombiwagen. Die haben doch allerhöchstens einen Morris Acht oder einen Austin Sieben.»

«Er will ja nur die Beine», erwiderte Rummins. «Wenn das übrige nicht hineingeht, kann er's hierlassen. Hauptsache, er hat die Beine, dann wird er schon zufrieden sein.»

«Das glauben Sie doch selbst nicht, Mr. Rummins», sagte Claud geduldig. «Sie wissen ganz genau, daß er vom Preis was abhandeln wird, wenn er nicht jedes kleine Stückchen mitkriegt. In Gelddingen sind alle Pfarrer gerieben, das steht nun mal fest. Und besonders dieser alte Knabe. Aber was halten Sie davon, wenn wir ihm sein Brennholz fix und fertig mitgeben? Wo haben Sie Ihre Axt?»

«Ja, das ist wohl das beste», meinte Rummins. «Los, Bert, hol die Axt her.»

Bert ging in den Schuppen und kam mit einer großen Holzfälleraxt zurück. Claud spuckte in die Hände, rieb sie aneinander, ergriff die Axt, schwang sie hoch in die Luft und ließ sie auf die beinlose Kommode niedersausen.

Die Arbeit war schwer, und es dauerte mehrere Minuten, bis er das Möbelstück kurz und klein geschlagen hatte.

«Eins kann ich euch sagen», verkündete er und wischte sich dabei den Schweiß von der Stirn. «Der Pfarrer mag reden, was er will, aber der Mann, der diese Kommode gebaut hat, war ein verflucht guter Tischler.»

«Wir haben's gerade noch geschafft», rief Rummins. «Da kommt er!»

Rummins came waddling over from the shed, squat and froglike, carrying a long saw. Claud took the saw away from him and went to work.

'Cut 'em close,' Rummins said. 'Don't forget he's going to use 'em on another table.'

The mahogany was hard and very dry, and as Claud worked, a fine red dust sprayed out from the edge of the saw and fell softly to the ground. One by one, the legs came off, and when they were all severed, Bert stooped down and arranged them carefully in a row.

Claud stepped back to survey the results of his labour. There was a longish pause.

'Just let me ask you one question, Mr Rummins,' he said slowly. 'Even now, could *you* put that enormous thing into the back of a car?'

'Not unless it was a van.'

'Correct!' Claud cried. 'And parsons don't have vans, you know. All they've got usually is piddling little Morris Eights or Austin Sevens.'

'The legs is all he wants,' Rummins said. 'If the rest of it won't go in, then he can leave it. He can't complain. He's got the legs.'

'Now you know better'n that, Mr Rummins,' Claud said patiently. 'You know damn well he's going to start knocking the price if he don't get every single bit of this into the car. A parson's just as cunning as the rest of 'em when it comes to money, don't you make any mistake about that. Especially this old boy. So why don't we give him his firewood now and be done with it. Where d'you keep the axe?'

'I reckon that's fair enough,' Rummins said. 'Bert, go fetch the axe.'

Bert went into the shed and fetched a tall woodcutter's axe and gave it to Claud. Claud spat on the palms of his hands and rubbed them together. Then, with a long-armed high-swinging action, he began fiercely attacking the legless carcass of the commode.

It was hard work, and it took several minutes before he had the whole thing more or less smashed to pieces.

'I'll tell you one thing,' he said, straightening up, wiping his brow: 'That was a bloody good carpenter put this job together and I don't care what the parson says.'

'We're just in time!' Rummins called out. 'Here he comes!'

Words and explanations

PAGE 5

theatre curtain	hier: *Theatervorstellung*
in other respects	*in anderen Punkten*
to throw sb into a state	*jdn in einen Zustand versetzen*
to twitch	*zucken*
vellicating muscle	*zuckender Muskel*
secret wink	*verstohlenes Blinzeln*
apprehension	*Besorgnis*
to flutter	*flattern*
to fidget	*zappeln*
to emerge from ...	*aus etw. herauskommen*
privacy	*Privatsphäre*
misery	*Elend*
mind you	*allerdings*
accurate	*genau*
bland	*nüchtern, kühl, vage*
to inflict sth on sb	*jdm etw. zufügen*
nasty	*boshaft*
to drive sb into hysterics	*jdn verrückt / hysterisch machen*
intensify	*verstärken*

PAGE 7

Assuming ...	hier: *Nehmen wir an ...*
attitude	*Haltung, Verhalten*
irrepressible	*unbezähmbar*
foible	hier: *Schwäche*
to torment	*quälen*

 six-storey house

In den USA wird das Erdgeschoss (**first floor**) meistens als erster Stock bezeichnet.
Ein **six-storey-house** in den USA entspricht also einem fünfstöckigen Haus bei uns.

 East Sixty-second Street

New York ist wie ein Gitter aufgeteilt – das heißt, die Straßen kreuzen im 90 Grad Winkel.
Wenn man die Stadt vom Flugzeug aus betrachtet, sieht man das Straßengitter. Viele große
Städte in den USA haben, vor allem im Stadtzentrum, diese Auteilung.

Manhattan ist in einen Ostteil (**East Side**) und einen Westteil (**West Side**) unterteilt. Die East Side grenzt an den East River und liegt auf der gegenüber liegenden Seite von Brooklyn und Queens. Die West Side grenzt an den Hudson River und liegt gegenüber New Jersey.

bustling	*belebt, voller Leben*
maid	*Dienstmädchen*
dust sheets	*Laken gegen Staub*
to drape	*drapieren, hängen*
to supervise	*beaufsichtigen*
study	*Arbeitszimmer*
luggage	*Gepäck*

 nine-fifteen

Statt **a quarter past nine** kann man auch **nine-fifteen** *(neun Uhr fünfzehn)* sagen.

to see sb off	*jdn verabschieden, jdn begleiten*

PAGE 9

to be fond of sb	*jdn gerne haben*
to dote on sb	*in jdn (ganz) vernarrt sein*
to stare	*starren*
disloyal	*illoyal*
to consent	*zustimmen*
intently	*aufmerksam, gespannt*
diminutive	*winzig, klein*
dapper	*adrett, elegant*
bearded	*mit Bart*

 Andrew Carnegie (1835 - 1919)

war ein amerikanischer Industrieller, der als Kind aus Schottland eingewandert war. Durch seine Investitionen in der Stahlindustrie wurde er sehr berühmt. Auf dem Gipfel seiner Karriere galt er als eine der einflussreichsten und wohlhabendsten Persönlichkeiten weltweit. Er unterstützte viele kulturelle Einrichtigen in den USA, wie z. B. die Carnegie Büchereien. Außerdem ließ er die nach ihm benannte Carnegie Hall errichten, in der bedeutende Konzerte stattfinden.

Words and explanations

PAGE 11

peculiar	*typisch, (eigen)tümlich*
to cock one's head	*den Kopf schräg legen*
jerk	*Ruck, Zuckung*
squirrel	*Eichhörnchen*
to sniff	*schnuppern*
foggy	*neblig*

Long Island

ist eine Insel im US-Bundesstaat New York, die sich von den Häfen der Stadt New York in den nördlichen Atlantik erstreckt. Die Insel, die etwa so groß wie Mallorca ist, ist sowohl bei Künstlern als auch bei wohlhabenden New Yorkern als Wohnsitz äußerst beliebt.

half-pay	*halber Lohn*

Club

Ein **Gentlemen's Club** war ursprünglich eine nur Mitgliedern vorbehaltene Vereinigung der englischen Oberschicht. Früher hatten nur Männer Zutritt, heute jedoch gibt es Tendenzen, sich auch für Frauen und Angehörige anderer sozialer Schichten zu öffnen.

Vor allem in London erfreuen sich Clubs heute wieder großer Beliebtheit. Sie bieten Essen, Trinken, eine angenehme Atmosphäre, die Möglichkeit zur Anmietung von Räumlichkeiten und oft auch Übernachtungsmöglichkeiten an.

occasionally	*ab und zu*
full wages	*voller Lohn*
to get up to	*etw. anstellen*
to snip off	*abknipsen*
cutter	*Zigarrenabschneider*
lighter	*Feuerzeug*
tight	*angespannt, fest*
rug	*Decke*

PAGE 13

Queen's Boulevard

ist eine der Hauptverkehrsadern im New Yorker Stadtteil Queens.

Idlewild

ist der frühere Name des New Yorker John F. Kennedy Flughafens.

to thicken	*dichter werden*
to fuss	*sich aufregen*
to be bound to ...	*müssen*
to observe	*wahrnehmen, bemerken*
to be in a rage	*vor Wut kochen, zornig sein*
to resign yourself to sth	*sich mit etw. abfinden*
to peer	*schauen, spähen*
muck	*Dreck, Mist*
to crawl	*kriechen*
on and on	*immer weiter*
to be stuck	*festsitzen*

PAGE **15**

disconsolate	*untröstlich*
to pushed one's way through	*sich einen Weg (durch die Menge) bahnen*
temporarily postponed	*vorübergehend verschoben*
to lean	*sich neigen, sich vorbeugen*
coarse	*rau, grob*
fur	*Pelz*
Have a good trip.	*Gute Reise!*
a sort of ...	*eine Art ...*
to wonder	*sich wundern*

(ABC) **to wonder**

Vorsicht Verwechslungsgefahr: **to wander** heißt *wandern*, **to wonder** bedeutet *sich wundern*.

hazy	*diesig, trüb*
in one way or another	*irgendwie*

eventually	*schließlich*

 eventually

Vorsicht! Lassen Sie sich nicht von diesem falschen Freund verleiten – **eventually** heißt nicht *eventuell,* sondern *schließlich, letztendlich.*

to take long	*lange dauern*
ridiculous	*lächerlich*

PAGE 17

In that case ...	*In diesem Fall ...*
to have sth at one's disposal	*etw. zu seiner Verfügung haben*
to make a fuss about sth	*viel Aufhebens um etw. machen*
definite	*endgültig, fest*
anxious	*unruhig*
bother to do sth	*sich die Mühe machen, etw. zu tun*
to drop sb at ...	*hier: jdn absetzen*
a long way off	*weit weg*
borderline	*Grenze*
to lie down	*sich hinlegen*

(ABC)

Vorsicht! Die Formen des Verbs **lie** *(liegen)* werden häufig mit den Verben **lie** *(lügen)* und **lay** *(legen)* verwechselt:

liegen: **lie – lay – lain** (-ing Form: **lying**)
lügen: **lie – lied – lied** (-ing Form: **lying**)
legen: **lay – laid – laid** (-ing Form: **laying**)

PAGE 19

purse	*Handtasche*
curiously cut	*seltsam geschnitten*

Edwardian

bezieht sich auf die „Edwardianische Phase" in der englischen Literatur (1901 – 1914). In England und Irland regierte in der Zeit König Edward VII.

lapel	*Aufschlag*
We'd better get going.	*Wir sollten langsam aufbrechen.*
goat	*Ziegenbock*
stovepipe trousers	*Röhrenhose*

(ABC) trousers

Achtung! Im Britischen Englisch ist *die Hose* (**trousers**) immer in der Mehrzahl. *Eine Hose* heißt **a pair of trousers**.

wisp	*Hauch, (kleines) Bündel*
behind the wheel	*am Steuer/Lenkrad*
Hold it a moment!	*Einen Moment!*
overcoat	*Mantel*
Where on earth is ...	*Wo um Himmels willen ...*
wrapped up in paper	*in Papier gewickelt*

PAGE 21

frantically	*verzweifelt, fieberhaft*
Confound it!	*Zum Teufel!*
for once	*ausnahmsweise (mal)*
to spot	*entdecken*
wedged down	*eingezwängt, eingekeilt*
couldn't help noticing that ...	*unwillkürlich feststellen müssen*
madly	*wie verrückt*
anxiety	*Angst*
spout	*Ausguss*
to be about to do sth	*im Begriff sein, etw. zu tun*
arrested	hier: *zum Stillstand gebracht*

Words and explanations

PAGE 23

tense	*angespannt*
repetition	*Wiederholung*
faintly	*schwach*
all at once	*plötzlich, auf einmal*
to withdraw	*zurücknehmen, zurückziehen*
to alter	*sich ändern*
hardness	*Härte*
flabby	*schlaff, schlapp*
authority	*Autorität*
cab	*Taxi*

 cab

ist ein anderes Wort für *Taxi*. In New York findet man die berühmten **yellow cabs**, die gelben Taxis. Der Autovermieter J.D Hertz ließ um 1900 seine Taxis gelb lackieren, damit diese besonders auffallen.

to urge sb to do sth	*darauf drängen, dass jd etw. tut*
a few minutes to spare	*hier: ein paar Minuten übrig*
to recline	*sich zurücklehnen*
hum	*Summen, Brummen*
to head for	*unterwegs sein nach*
mood	*Stimmung*
remarkably	*außergewöhnlich*
queer	*eigenartig, seltsam*
a trifle	*ein wenig*
breathless	*außer Atem, atemlos*
sense of calmness	*Gefühl der Ruhe/Gelassenheit*
in the flesh	*in echt, in natura*

PAGE 25

chatty	*geschwätzig*
gossip	*Klatsch*
to hint at sth	*etw. andeuten, auf etw. hinweisen*
in not too distant future	*in nicht allzu ferner Zukunft*
to overstay one's time	*hier: länger als vorgesehen bleiben*

to send a cable to	*ein Telegramm schicken an* (veraltet)
to be interested to observe	*mit Interesse feststellen*
to overtip sb	*jdm zu viel Trinkgeld geben*
porter	*Träger*
baggage	*Gepäck*

 baggage – luggage

Gepäck heißt in den USA **baggage**, in Großbritannien sagt man **luggage**.

lump	*Klumpen*
gutter	*Abflussgraben, Gosse*
to tinkle shrilly	*schrill klingeln*
pantry	*Vorratskammer*
pile	*Haufen, Stapel*
oppressive	*drückend, beklemmend*
faint	*schwach*
odour	*Geruch*
deliberate	*beabsichtigt, bewusst*
purposeful	*zielbewusst, entschlossen*
rumour	*Gerücht*
glimmer	*Schimmer*

° PAGE 27

indicator	*Anzeige(r)*
right away	*sofort*
patiently	*geduldig*

° PAGE 29

parson	*Pfarrer*
primrose	*Schlüsselblume*
hawthorn	*Hagedorn*
hedge	*Hecke*
underneath	*darunter*

Words and explanations

a clump of flowers	hier: *Büschel Blumen*
cluster	*Gruppe*
summit	*Gipfel*
elevation	*Erhebung*
outskirts of the village	*Rand des Dorfes*
pad	*Zeichenblock*
track	*Weg*
elm	*Ulme*

 Queen Anne

bezieht sich auf eine Stilrichtung in britischer und US-amerikanischer Architektur des späten 19. Jahrhunderts.

rough sketch	*grobe Skizze*

 Georgian

Der Georgianische Stil ist ein Architekturstil, der in den englischsprachigen Ländern zwischen ca. 1720 und 1840 verbreitet war. Diese Stilrichtung bezieht sich vor allem auf die Klassik der Griechen und Römer, was sich hauptsächlich bei den Fassaden bemerkbar macht.

binoculars	*Fernglas*
prosperous	*wohlhabend*
well ordered	hier: *in bester Ordnung*

PAGE **31**

to rule sth out	*etw. ausschließen*
to call on sb	*jdn besuchen*
square	hier: *Abschnitt*

 a pint of beer

In England, Schottland, Wales und Irland wird das Bier in Pubs in **pints** ausgeschenkt. Ein „Pint" entspricht 0,568 l.

dilapidated	*verfallen*
... could do with ...	*könnte ... gebrauchen*

to release the handbrake	*die Handbremse lösen*
to cruise	hier: *rollen*
disguised	*verkleidet*
clergyman	*Geistlicher*
sinister	*unheimlich, drohend*
by trade	*von Beruf*
showroom	*Ausstellungsraum*

 King's Road, Chelsea

Die King's Road im Stadtteil Chelsea ist eine bekannte und exklusive Einkaufsstraße im Londoner Westen.

premises	*Geschäftsräume*
to sell sth dear	*etw. teuer verkaufen*
tidy income	*nettes Einkommen*
to suit	*passen*
grave	*ernst*
the aged	*die Bejahrten*
obsequious	*untertänig, unterwürfig*
sober	*nüchtern, schlicht*
the godly	*die Frommen*
masterful	*herrisch*
mischievous	*schelmisch*
arch	*verschmitzt*
saucy	*frech*
spinster	*alte Jungfer*
gift	*Talent*
shamelessly	*schamlos*
to turn aside	hier: *vortreten*
to take a bow	*sich verbeugen*
thundering applause	*donnernder Applaus*
clownish quality	*närrische Eigenschaft*
ungraceful	*ohne Anmut*
genuine	*echt*

PAGE **33**

to achieve fame	*Ruhm erwerben*
considerable	*beträchtlich*
astonishing	*erstaunlich*
apparently	*anscheinend*
source of supply	*Quelle*
inexhaustible	*unerschöpflich*
warehouse	*Warenlager*
to smile knowingly	*überlegen lächeln*
to wink	*zwinkern*
to murmur	*murmeln*

 Sevenoaks

ist eine Stadt im Einzugsgebiet von London. Sie liegt in der Grafschaft Kent und ist ca. 35 km vom Zentrum entfernt, so dass viele Pendler sich dort niedergelassen haben.

fan belt	*Keilriemen*
to overheat	*überhitzen*
smallish	*(recht) klein*
sweat	*schwitzen*
oak	*Eiche*
panel	hier: *Rückenlehne*
beautifully turned spindles	*wundervoll gedrechselte Spindeln*
inlay	*Einlegearbeit*
floral design	*Blumenmuster*
carved	*geschnitzt*
half the length	*Hälfte*
to poke one's head through ...	*den Kopf durch ... stecken*
By heavens!	hier: *Du meine Güte!*
straight away	*geradeaus, ohne Umschweife*
Why on earth ...	*Warum in aller Welt ...*
to be willing to do sth	*bereit sein, etw. zu tun*
definitely	hier: *ganz bestimmt*
out of curiosity	*aus Neugier*

PAGE 35

couldn't do without sth	*etw. nicht entbehren können*
all the same	*trotzdem*
Call it ...	hier: *Sagen wir ...*
to bargain	*handeln*
a twentieth of	*ein Zwanzigstel von*
value	*Wert*
station-wagon	*Kombiwagen*
fabulous	*fabelhaft*
tucked away	*untergebracht, versteckt*
snugly	hier: *gut*
to be struck by an idea	*eine Idee haben*
to interfere	*stören*
large-scale map	*Karte mit großem Maßstab*
county	*Grafschaft*

 county

Grafschaften (**counties**) sind Gebiets-/Verwaltungseinheiten in Großbritannien. In der Nähe von London befinden sich z. B. die Grafschaften Kent, Surrey und Hertfordshire.

to estimate	*schätzen*
cope with	hier: *etw. erledigen*
thoroughly	*gründlich*
comparatively	*vergleichsweise*
mansion	*Herrenhaus*
gradually	*nach und nach*
a suspicious lot	*misstrauischer Haufen*
impoverished	*verarmt*
to show sb around one's house	*jdm sein Haus zeigen*
just for the asking	*einfach so*
to gain admittance	*Einlass erhalten*
plumber	*Klempner*
scheme	*Plan*
to take on a more practical aspect	*konkreter werden*
a large quantity	*eine große Menge*
superior	hier: *ausgezeichnet*

card	*Visitenkarte*
engraved	*geprägt*

° PAGE 37

reverend	*Pfarrer/Hochwürden*
preservation	*Erhaltung*
in association with	*in Gemeinschaft mit*
from now on	*von nun an*
a labour of love	*Liebesdienst*
to compile	*zusammenstellen*
inventory	*Inventar*
to kick sb out	*jemanden hinauswerfen*
to one's surprise	*zu jemandes Überraschung*
slice	*Stück*
pie	*Pastete, Kuchen*

 pie

ist ein im gesamten englischsprachigen Raum sehr beliebtes Gericht. Es handelt sich hierbei um ein Gebäck, das mit süßen (z. B. **apple pie**) oder herzhaften (z. B. **chicken and mushroom pie**) Füllungen versehen wird.

port	*Portwein*

 port

ist ein relativ süßer und schwerer Likörwein aus Portugal. Er war ab dem 18. Jahrhundert in Großbritannien sehr beliebt und es gibt einige Trinkrituale, die ihren Ursprung in der Seefahrt haben.

plum	*Pflaume*
to press sth upon sb	*jdm etw. aufdrängen*
quantity	*Menge*
lucrative business	*lukratives Geschäft*
to operate	*betätigen*

Buckinghamshire

ist eine Grafschaft im mittleren Südengland, ca. 60 km nordwestlich von London gelegen. Sie grenzt u. a. an die Grafschaft Oxfordshire.

yard	*Yard*

 yard

ist eine Längeneinheit des angloamerikanischen Maßsystems und entspricht 91,44 Zentimetern.

to examine sth closely	*etw. genau untersuchen*
suitable for the occasion	*dem Anlass entsprechend*

· ·

PAGE 39

· ·

to stride briskly	*schnell schreiten*
fat-legged	*mit dicken Schenkeln*
to bulge out	*hervorquellen*
imbecility	*Dummheit*
dog-collar	*Hundehalsband*
to lend sb an air	*jdm ein Aussehen von … verleihen*
rustic	*rustikal*
easy-going	*gemächlich, gelassen*
riding-breeches	*Reithosen*
stable	*Stall*
horse manure	*Pferdemist*
to cling	*anhaften*
suspiciously	*misstrauisch*
whinny	*wiehern*

 the Socialist Party

Die Sozialistische Partei ist eine marxistische politische Partei in England und Wales.

pale	*blass, hell*
bushy brows	*buschige Augenbrauen*

Tory

So wird ein Mitglied der Konservativen Partei des britischen Parlaments bezeichnet.

a sitting duck	*leichte Beute*
to deliver an eulogy	*eine Lobrede halten*
impassioned	*begeistert*

 the Conservative Party

ist eine Konservative Partei in Großbritannien, die sich 1830 aus der Gruppierung „Tory Party" gebildet hat. Die Konservativen werden daher heute als Tories bezeichnet. Die Partei wird oft auch als Right Wing bezeichnet.

to denounce	*verurteilen, anprangern*
clincher	*Trumpf*
to made a reference to	*sich beziehen auf*
bill	*Gesetzentwurf*
abolition of blood sports	hier: *Verbot von Hetzjagden*
stag	*Hirsch*
hare	*Hase*
pack of hounds	*Hundemeute*
tireless	*unermüdlich*
morn	*Morgen*
guffaw of laughter	*schallendes Gelächter*
to slap sb	*jdn schlagen*

PAGE 41

barren	*unfruchtbar, karg*
to take one's leave	*(weg) gehen*
half-timbered	*Fachwerk*
brick building	*Ziegelgebäude*
of considerable age	*von beträchtlichem Alter*
pear tree	*Birnbaum*
in blossom	*in Blüte*
cowshed	*Kuhstall*
alcove	*Nische*

semicircular	*halbrund*
card-table	*Spieltisch*
mahogany	*Mahagoni*
richly veneered	*prächtig/reich furniert*

 George Hepplewhite

war ein englischer Kunsttischler im 18. Jahrhundert und berühmt für seine zierlichen Stühle und Tische mit leicht geschwungenen Linien.

lattice	*Gitter*
honeysuckle	*Geißblatt*
husk	*Schote*
paterae	*Blumenrelief*
caning	*Geflecht*
gracefully	*anmutig*
outward splay	hier: *Schwung nach außen*
exquisite	*erlesen*
to have the pleasure of doing sth	*die Freude haben, etw. zu tun*
intriguing sight	*faszinierender Anblick*
to gauge	*beurteilen*
infinitesimal	*winzig*
shrinkage	hier: *Nachgeben*
mortice	*Fugen*
dovetail joints	*Schwalbenschwanzverbindungen*
back yard	*Hinterhof*

···

° PAGE **43**

···

to hold out hope	*sich etw. erhoffen*
rambling	*wuchernd*
in bad repair	*in schlechtem Zustand*
greyhound	*Windhund*
leash	*Leine*
to catch sight of	*jemanden sehen*
to stiffen	*erstarren*
stumpy	*untersetzt*

shifty eyes	*verschmitzte Augen*
corrugated brow	*gerunzelte Stirn*
pork	*Schweinefleisch*
ham	*Schinken*
government permit	*behördliche Genehmigung*
to poke one's nose into sth	*herumschnüffeln*
peculiar expression	*eigenartiger Gesichtsausdruck*
jeer	*höhnen, spotten*
contemptuous curl	*geringschätziges Kräuseln*
sneer	*Hohn, Spott*

○ PAGE 45

to swivel	*schwenken*
aim	*Ziel*
to waste one's time	*seine Zeit vergeuden*
dirty-looking	*schmutzig*
worth four hundred pound	*vierhundert Pfund wert*
primly	*steif*
ladder	*Leiter*
hobnailed boots	*genagelte Schuhe*
to pry	*stöbern, spionieren*
larder	*Speisekammer*
wicked eyes	*boshafte Augen*
to go to the trouble	*sich die Mühe machen*
to take a fancy	*an etw. Gefallen finden*
beyond my means	*es übersteigt meine Mittel*
to be tempted to do sth	*versucht sein, etw. zu tun*
But alas, ...	*Aber leider ...*

○ PAGE 47

deal table	*Tisch zum Kartenspielen*
exceedingly filthy	*außerordentlich schmutzig*
to stop dead in one's tracks	*wie angewurzelt stehen bleiben*

solid	*solide, wirklich*
admittedly	*zugegeben*
to stripe off	*entfernen*
in any event	*in jedem Fall, auf jeden Fall*
to spoil	*verderben*
in a flash	*plötzlich*
to stagger	*taumeln*
fatuous leer	*blödes Starren*
a fraction	*Stückchen*
crafty grin	*ausgefuchstes Grinsen*
stub	*Stummel*
to compose oneself	*sich sammeln, sich zusammenreißen*

○ **PAGE 49**

to keep calm	*ruhig bleiben*
wary	*wachsam*
sly	*gerissen*
to peek through	*hindurch spähen*
the slightest doubt	*der geringste Zweifel*
layman	*Laie*
coveted example	*begehrtes Exemplar*
in existence	*vorhanden*

 Sotheby's

ist eines der bekanntesten und ältesten Auktionshäuser der Welt; es wurde 1744 vom Buchhändler Samuel Baker in London gegründet.

to turn up	*auftauchen*
to fetch enormous prices	*enorme Preise erzielen*
veneer	*Furnier*
log	*Holzblock*
set of templates	*Musterreihe*
invoice	*Rechnung*
to execute	*ausführen*

Words and explanations

 Thomas Chippendale

war ein bedeutender Kunsttischler des 18. Jahrhunderts. Der Chippendale-Stil, der oft als „englisches Rokoko" bezeichnet wird, wurde nach ihm benannt.

exalted	*überschwänglich*
to go down in history	*in die Geschichte eingehen*

° PAGE 51

luscious offer	*großartiges Angebot*

 West End

ist das Londoner Theaterviertel.

 The Times

ist eine nationale Tageszeitung aus Großbritannien. Die bekannte Schrift „Times (New) Roman" wurde 1931 für die Zeitung entwickelt.

to make a stir	*Aufsehen erregen*

 rococo style

Das Rokoko ist eine kulturgeschichtliche Epoche, die eine Weiterentwicklung des Barock darstellt (ca. 1720 bis 1775). Typisch für den Rokoko-Stil sind kunstvolle Verzierungen und die Aufgabe von Symmetrie, die im Barock noch ein wichtiges Element war.

chest-of-drawers	*Kommode*
fluted	*gerillt, geriffelt*
drawer	*Schublade*
magnificently ornamented	*reich verziert*
vertically	*senkrecht*
intricate carvings	*kunstvolle Schnitzereien*
festoon	*Girlande*
scroll	*Spirale*
brass handle	*Messinggriff*
partly obscured	*teilweise überdeckt*
grace	*Anmut*

offensive	*störend, anstößig*
unsteadily	*wackelig, schwankend*
flip	hier: *Antippen*
crude reproduction	*plumpe Imitation*

PAGE 53

craftsmanship	*handwerkliches Können*
to saunter off	*weiter schlendern*
to frown	*die Stirn runzeln*
to trail off	*allmählich verstummen*

 Michaelmas

Der Michaelstag (**Michaelmas**) ist der Festtag des Hl. Michael am 29. September.

mover	*Möbelpacker*
sermon	*Predigt*
mistrusting	*misstrauisch*
boiled	*gesotten*
misty	hier: *verschwommen*
dot	*Punkt*

 Manor House

Als *Herrenhaus* (**manor house**) bezeichnet man vom Landadel oder Großgrundbesitzern bewohnte Gebäude.

squire	*Gutsherr*
vacantly	*leer, geistig abwesend*

PAGE 55

to utter a sound	*einen Laut von sich geben*
literally	*buchstäblich*
plump	*dick*
hen	*Henne*
stray	*vereinzelt*

grains of corn	*Getreidekörner*
rabbit-snares	*Kaninchenschlingen*
to dip	*eintauchen*
to rummage	*herumwühlen*
string	*Schnüre*
to unfold	*entfalten*
brittle	*spröde*
to crack	*knistern*
in a sloping hand	*in schräger Schrift*
copperplate	*gestochen*
exceeding	*außergewöhnlich*
to hold to oneself tight	*sich beherrschen*
to suppress	*unterdrücken*
to spin round	*sich im Kreis drehen*
dizzy	*schwindlig*
to toss sth on the table	*etw. auf den Tisch werfen*
to pass sth off as	*etw. verkaufen als*
to give the game away	*ausplaudern, sich verraten*

PAGE 57

cabinet-maker	*Kunsttischler*
to fake	*imitieren*
to gather round	*sich um etw. versammeln*
horn-handled	*mit Horngriff*
apparent casualness	*scheinbar nachlässig*
to chip off	*abkratzen*
to flake away	*abblättern*
varnish	*Lack*
topaz	*Topas*
processed	*behandelt*
chiefly	*hauptsächlich*
without the slightest doubt	*ohne den leisesten Zweifel*
lime	*Leim*
aged	hier: *gealtert*
potash salt	*Pottasche*

walnut	*Walnuss*
nitric acid	*Salpetersäure*
stirring of interest	*Erwecken von Interesse*
cookery	*Schwindel*
grain	*Maserung*
touch of sth	*Hauch von etw.*
patina	*Patina*

○ PAGE 59

as applied to	*in Bezug auf*
rascal	*Schuft*
to spit	*spucken, speien*
a mortal	*Sterbliche/r*
deceive	*betrügen*
linseed oil	*Leinöl*
to coat sth over	*etw. auftragen*
cunningly	*schlau*
to brush sth down	*etw. abbürsten*
pumice-stone	*Bimsstein*
to beeswax	*mit Bienenwachs einreiben*
wax	*Wachs*
knavery	*Schurkerei*
to be cold to the touch	*sich kalt anfühlen*
finger-tip	*Fingerspitze*
to pass a judgement	*ein Urteil abgeben*
barley	*Gerste*
handle	*Handgriff*

○ PAGE 61

to be none the wiser	*nicht schlauer sein*
to rust	*rosten*
scoundrel	*Schuft, Schurke*
to come in handy	*sich als nützlich erweisen*
shaving	*Späne*

Words and explanations

PAGES 61 – 67

saturated	hier: *getränkt*
sal ammoniac	*Salmiak*
to rub off	*abreiben*
lustre	*Glanz*
hinge	*Scharnier*
pitted	*vernarbt*
in no time	*nach kurzer Zeit*
screwdriver	*Schraubenzieher*
screw	*Schraube*
spiral	*Gewinde*
uneven	*unregelmäßig*
to substitute	*ersetzen*
rewarding	*belohnend*

° PAGE 63

to be stocked with	*ausgestattet sein mit*
evenness	*Gleichmäßigkeit*
ironmonger's	*Eisenwarenhändler*
to peep	*einen kurzen Blick auf etw. werfen*
old bore	*alter Langweiler*
to part with	*sich von etw. trennen*
to shrug one's shoulders	*mit den Schultern zucken*
scornful	*verächtlich*
to stab	*stechen*
fore-finger	*Zeigefinger*
reckless	*leichtsinnig*

° PAGE 65

quiver	*Schauer*
needle	*Nadel*
sole	*Sohle*
necessity	*Notwendigkeit*
to give in	*zustimmen, aufgeben*

carcass	*Gestell, Gerippe*
to haggle	*feilschen*
in a jiffy	*im Handumdrehen, gleich*
uncontrollably	*hemmungslos*
bubble	*Blase*
to burst	*platzen*
buttercup	*Butterblume*

 sovereign

ist eine ehemalige englische Goldmünze im Wert von 1 Pfund. Der **Sovereign** wird gern gesammelt bzw. als Geldanlage genutzt, er ist aber auch heute noch formal gültiges Zahlungsmittel.

to be littered with sth	*übersät mit*
to swing off	*abweichen, ausschwingen*
to tread on sth	*zertreten*
tinkle	*Klimpern*

PAGE 67

Fancy ...	*Stellt euch/Stellen Sie sich vor ...*
To hell with it.	*Zum Teufel damit.*
to be keen on sth	*von etw. angetan sein*
prospect	*Aussicht*
relentlessly	*unbarmherzig*
on the spot	*hier, an Ort und Stelle*
bovine face	*Rindsgesicht*
mawkish pride	hier: *dummer Stolz*
saw	*Säge*
cow dung	*Kuhmist*
to conduct oneself	*sich benehmen*
to break into a trot	*in einen Trab fallen*
hop	*hüpfen*
skip	*springen*

Words and explanations

○ PAGE **69**

reckon	*meinen*
balmy	*verrückt*
socket	hier: *Augenhöhle*
to waddle	*watscheln*
shed	*Schuppen*
squat	*plump*
to spray	*sprühen*
to survey	*betrachten*
van	*Transporter*
piddling	*lächerlich*

 Morris Eights und Austin Sevens

waren britische Kleinwagen der 20er und 30er Jahre.

to knock the price	*den Preis runterhandeln*
cunning	*gerissen*
axe	*Axt*
woodcutter	*Holzfäller*
fiercely	*hcftig*
to smash sth to pieces	*etw. in Stücke schlagen*
to wipe	*wischen*
carpenter	*Tischler*

Roald Dahl – mehr als nur gute Geschichten ...

Wussten Sie, dass 10 % der Autorentantiemen* aus diesem Buch an die Roald Dahl Wohltätigkeitsorganisationen gehen?

Die **Roald Dahl Stiftung** unterstützt Fachkinderkrankenschwestern, die sich im gesamten Vereinigten Königreich um Kinder mit Epilepsie, Blutkrankheiten und erworbenen Hirnschäden kümmern.

Außerdem bietet sie praktische Unterstützung für Kinder und Jugendliche mit Hirn- und Bluterkrankungen sowie Lese- und Rechtschreibschwäche (dies lag Roald Dahl bereits zu Lebzeiten sehr am Herzen) durch Zuschüsse an Krankenhäuser und Wohltätigkeitsorganisationen und an einzelne Kinder und Familien.

Das **Roal Dahl Museum and Story Centre** befindet sich in Great Missenden vor den Toren Londons, dem Dorf in Buckinghamshire, in dem Roald Dahl arbeitete und lebte. Das einzigartige Archiv von Briefen und Manuskripten bildet das Herzstück des Museums, das zum Lesen und Schreiben animieren soll. Neben zwei amüsanten biografischen Galerien bietet das Museum auch ein interaktives Geschichtszentrum. Hier können Familien, Lehrer und ihre Schüler die aufregende Welt der Kreativität und des Schreibens entdecken.

www.roalddahlfoundation.org

www.roalddahlmuseum.org

Die *Roald Dahl Foundation* (RDF) ist eine eingetragene Wohltätigkeitsorganisation, No. 1004230.

Das *Roald Dahl Museum and Story Centre* (RDMSC) ist eine eingetragene Wohltätigkeitsorganisation, No. 1085853.

Der *Roald Dahl Charitable Trust* ist eine neue Wohltätigkeitsorganisation, die die Arbeit von RDF und RDMSC unterstützt.

* gespendete Tantiemen sind provisionsfrei

LESEN UND HÖREN SIE AUCH ANDERE TITEL AUS DER REIHE!

READ & LISTEN

Dave Eggers, The Only Meaning of the Oil-Wet Water
ISBN: 978-3-12-**561545**-8

Jonathan Franzen, My Father's Brain
ISBN: 978-3-12-**561547**-2

Nick Hornby, 6 Songs
ISBN: 978-3-12-**561542**-7

Marian Keyes, Twelve Months
ISBN: 978-3-12-**561546**-5

Stephen King, The Jaunt
ISBN: 978-3-12-**561555**-7

Ian Rankin, Playback
ISBN: 978-3-12-**561549**-6

Muriel Spark, The Portobello Road
ISBN: 978-3-12-**561541**-0

www.pons.de